Sucker4Pain Vol. 2:

Pain, Love prisons, and the Fight for Redemption

By

Coolgmack

Copyright © 2025 by Jaron burnett

All rights reserved. No part of this publication may be reproduced, stored in a retrieval system, or transmitted in any form or by any means—electronic, mechanical, photocopying, recording, or otherwise—without the prior written permission of the author, except in the case of brief quotations used in critical articles or reviews.
This book is a work of original expression. All poems, reflections, and narratives are based on the author's lived experience, creative vision, and social commentary. Any resemblance to actual persons, living or dead, or actual events is purely intentional.
Unauthorized use, duplication, or distribution of this work is a violation of applicable laws and will be pursued to the fullest extent.

Isbn:**979-8-9930046-6-2**

Published in the United States.

Cover design and layout by Coolgmack

Contact/Website: Coolgmack.com

coolgmack@gmail.com   @coolgmack on all platforms

"The hardest thing in life is letting go of what you thought was real." — Juice WRLD

Foreword

When I first picked up a pen, I was in the ruins—broken promises, silent phones, bed sheets soaked in regret and gloom. I wrote to survive the lonely nights I couldn't sleep and to rebuild when the world said I was done and a creep.

Sucker4Pain 2 is my truth. Every scar I swallowed. Every pride I dropped. Every moment I stood back up.

In these pages, you'll find my heart—opened, closed, chipped. This isn't just my story. It's the testament of anyone who's loved the wrong one, fought the system, lost their way, and still found the road back to themselves.

It's my heart calling out for help. My body being released from her grip. All the painful pleasures I felt. Being hurt but carrying pain in silence.

I'm just a sucker for love that became a sucker for pain—addicted to the emotions and commotions stuck in my veins.

This is my testimony.

Coolgmack

Dedication

To God, first and foremost—for being there through the ups and downs and the down-downs. You never gave up on me, even when I gave up on You. Thank You for the grace I've been given and for shielding me from death time and time again.

To my family—who showed love regardless of my mental health struggles. Y'all know who you are. I see you. I love you.

To all the women who gave me content to write about—the lessons were painful, but necessary. Thank you for being part of my testimony.

To everyone who tried to drown me—I guess you didn't know you can't sink a vessel that's Holy.

To all my brothers and sisters locked up—do the time, don't let the time do you. Make it count. Be productive. Don't let depression and oppression get the best of you. Your story isn't over.

To my old friends I had to leave behind—my bad, but I had to change, and that meant changing my circle too. If you decide to grow with me, we can reconnect. I can't afford negativity anymore. I don't have any more time to give to prison—mental or physical. This book is proof: survival is possible. Redemption is real. And you are not your past.

Foreword..4

Dedication..6

Chapter 1: Through the Veil.............................1

Through the Veil..3

The Queen's Betrayal...5

Chipped crown..11

The Weight I Won't Carry..................................13

I Refuse to Sink...15

Mirror Truth...17

Chapter 2: The Fallouts....................................19

Lost, Confused, & Listening to Otis................21

Left in the Rain..25

Elusive dreams 2...27

Betrayed but not Broken.................................33

💔 Cryonyx 2: A Second Chance.....................37

Ex-ploding...41

Crash course...43

Chapter 3: Flesh and Fire................................47

Flesh Without Fire...49

Microwave love...51

Frozen Desire..55

Survived the Fire...59

Hula Hoops..63

Burning thru the furnace.................................65

Heaven-Sent and Hell-Bent.............................67

Chapter 4: Ghosted by Love............................69

Hollow Gestures..71

Cold call...73

A love/hate Dance..77

Duck Duck Goose...79

Family Tithes..83

♥ 🤜 (heartfist)..87

I Thought We Were Cool...................................91

Love skitzo..95

End Zone Dreams..101

   Chapter 5: Love's Illusions..........................105

I dunno...107

I dunno what it is...113

No Calls, No Mail...117

Sixth Inning Switch...123

Not Worth It...125

   Chapter 6: Unwavering..................................129

Unwavering..131

Rising From the Ashes..135

Child of God..139

Refined...141

   Chapter 7: Deliverance..................................145

Convicted to Affliction..147

My Own Worst Enemy..151

Caged by Deception..155

Domestic terrorists...159

No Third Party..161

Raft in the Ocean...165

   Chapter 8: Revolving Doors..........................169

Revolving whore/door...171

999th Attempt...179

The 1000th Truth..183

Thank You for The Pain.......................................185

About Author...189

More books by Coolgmack....................................191

Chapter 1: Through the Veil

Seeing the truth beyond deception — the awakening.

"Peeling back the masks, seeing what's real through the lies. This chapter is about waking up to betrayal, facing the shadows, and beginning to trust your own eyes."

Through the Veil

I see through the veil you wove with ease,
Each thread a falsehood spun to please
You alone—no thought, no care
For trust that hung suspended there.

Your deception grows its twisted roots,
Unflinching as it bears its fruits
Of distance, doubt, and hollow space
Where once I saw an honest face.

The lies you told without a blink,
So callous that I cannot think
How easily the words were said,

How little weight each promise weighed.
Yet I stand firm against the storm,
Your shifting truths, your shapeless form
I know now what I have to do:
Place oceans wide between me and you.

This misplaced faith I once held dear
Now crystallizes, cold and clear
Not bitterness, but knowing sight:
Some distances are set for flight.

I weather this with steady breath,
This small rehearsal before a death
Of what we were, of what we're not
The garden grew from seeds of rot.

So let your falsehoods find new ground,
Let other hearts be tightly bound
By stories that you spin at will
I've walked away. I'm walking still.

The Queen's Betrayal

She was supposed to be my queen,
The one who knelt before me
And promised me eternity
But hid betrayal in her spleen.
Like a thief of my dreams.

She swore to protect me,
But instead dissected me,
Crossed my chest selectively
Like a pawnless rookie,
Stormed my castle,
Took everything,
Left my mind battling her shadows.

Scars? Internal.
Etched like ink under my skin
Never fading, always burning.
They say you are what you eat,
So maybe I was weak, maybe I was soft,
But even lions cry when love turns its claws.

Still, I won't cry in the rain.
Where the thunder listens.
I'll keep it pimpin' like Ken's dressing.

Dripping in pain
But wearing it like chains,
Too saucy to be salty,
Too stubborn to break the pane
I won't let her remember
Become a recession in my soul.
This time,
I move in silence, calculating—cold,
Because I finally know
She ain't ever going to change.
It's evident in her absence,
In her actions, which are vain
She danced around my dignity.
And called it love. I call it pain.

Strange how I let it happen,
How I entertained
The circus and became a clown.
But at least I know now

No more roles, no more shows
No more friends.
I run like presidents
When your name reaches my residence,
Because baby, your energy is lethal,
And I'm done inhaling it.

Your game is seen through

You've been fired, expired,
The liar I once admired.
The heartbreak? I can consider.
But the poison still lingers.
Dripping slowly from within,
Like venom under my skin.
And still, I smile.

Still, I pray.
Still, I move.
Even though you crooked my grin
Like a dentist with a vendetta,
Though you meant for this to ruin me,
You failed better.

You left me in the cold
And now I'm half the man,
But with twice the vision.
Real loyalty, real strength.
Your fake love taught me
How to spot the real thing.

No—I won't go to war with you.
I won't battle someone

Who already knew
They lost me.
Keep your non-apologies;
They bounce right off me.
I forgive myself
Forever thinking your love was holy.

I don't need closure from you
I just need distance.
So I can dispose of you
You took my heart and apprehended it.
Like it was nothing,
Like it wasn't beating for you.
Pushed all my buttons
I never cheated on you

The jewels you gave were fake.
Just like the promises.
Just like the "forevers."
Just like the way you vow to give.
You were handing the kitty
To another man like it was candy.
That was supposed to be only my pantry.

But it's all good.
I won't curse your name

I'll forget about you.
I'll pretend we never happened.
No more friends,
No more fake mending.
I stayed past my limit,
But grace got me through it.

God pulled me from your fire,
And I still breathe
You can try, but
You can't count me out,
Not with fingers, not with toes. Not me!

So wash your face,
Miss me with your guilt trips.
Mrs. Misery,
Your silence is finally a gift.

I'm sorry, I'm not sorry
That I won't be the better man.
I regret this—all of it.
Every lie, every second, every kiss.

You had me looking goofy and crazy,
A fool in a mirror
Cracking under pressure,

Trying to heal from a wound
That you kept pressing.

My trust was your playground,
And you built nothing but illusions.
You even convinced me it was me.
That I was the problem,
And you were the solution

That I was the flaw in the mirror,
While you stood there flawless,
Projecting poison with a perfume
Smiling and adoring all of this

But no more.
This was your final move,
Your last act,
Your goodbye with glitter.
And me? I survived. But bitter

This is my checkmate.
Not in love, but in truth.
And this king didn't die on the floor.
He rises past your roof.

Chipped crown

Wow...
You couldn't even wait 8 months for me to come home.
Guess that was way too much
To ask, the word around town was...
You're showing a brand-new baby bump
That doesn't belong to me.
Of course, I was mad.

When I first heard it,
I was touched
And crazy stumped.
The news hit my stomach like a punch,
Out of nowhere...
Don't even go there.
You didn't just get pregnant by accident or cold air.
You ain't Mary, and you sure ain't no virgin
We were supposed to get married,
Build something holy,
But you submerged our purpose.
In someone else's ocean.

Now when I come home,
I'll be walking into silence alone.
No ring,

No throne,
Just a king
Learning how to rebuild his own.

I hope it was worth it.
Whatever moment broke the promise.
Now our love story fades.
Behind heavy curtains.

But I'm coming home
To be a better person
Stronger,
Sober, wiser
And certainly.

Take care.
And just to clear the air...
I was loyal to you.
Always sincere.
But you...
You just don't care.
Now I'm out of here.
My heart still hurts. It ain't fair.

The Weight I Won't Carry

You took my hours like a thief takes a theft
silently, certain, leaving less than death.
I circled your labyrinths, learned your twisted turns,
counted all the time a trusting heart burns.

But bitterness? No. I refuse that throne.
I've walked through fire and claimed myself, alone.
I've sat with doctors of the mind and the soul,
excavated pieces, slowly becoming whole.

Forgiveness lives somewhere in my chest
not for you, but so that I can truly rest.
It doesn't mean I've forgotten what you've done,
doesn't mean your poison and my peace are one.

You are my jinx, my curse, my chaos czar,
the one who pushed me toward the edge too far.
I stood at the rail of a ship taking water,
watched you drill the holes, heard the hull's last slaughter.

But I am not drowning. I am not your wreck.
I am the survivor on the upper deck,
who learned to swim in seas you tried to claim,
who built a raft from splinters of your shame.
You meant to break me. I refused to fall.
And that, my karma, is my freedom after all.

I Refuse to Sink

Despite the time
the energy lost,
the nights I bled into dawn
trying to decode your chaos
I refuse.

I refuse to bow to bitterness.
You twisted the truth,
played puppeteer with peace,
But I've learned to cut the strings
with my own healing hands.
I will not see defeat

I sought solace
in the silence of therapy rooms,
in ink-stained journals,
in the mirror of my own mind.
I escaped your inferno

I stitched myself together
with words,
with wisdom,
with will.
With forgiveness

Yes, it's within reach.
But don't mistake my grace
for ignorance.
Don't mistake my peace
for permission.
You are not so innocent

I see you.
My jinx.
My harbinger of discord.
You pushed me
to the jagged edge
of my own sword

Whispered of ruin
as the ship began to tilt.
But listen
I am not sinking.
I am the sea.
I am the storm.
I am tough built
And every wave
that tried to drown me
now carries my name
as a warning
I rise. I rise. I rise.

Mirror Truth

Lately I've been staring in the mirror,
Seeing what she can't see,
Asking if I'm the problem.

Am I too much? Not enough?
Do I love too hard, trust too quick?
I see a man who's willing to fight,
But maybe the battle was never mine to win.

I see value she overlooked,
Potential she couldn't recognize,
A heart she wasn't ready to hold.

The mirror shows me the truth
I'm not the problem,
I'm the lesson she wasn't ready to fold.

And that's when everything got clearer,
When I stopped trying to make her see
And started seeing myself differently.

Chapter 2: The Fallouts

Aftermath — heartbreak, betrayal, and the emotional wreckage left behind

"When the walls crumble and the storms hit, you're left with the pieces that leave you unwhole. Pain, regret, and anger collide here—the fallout of love gone wrong and lessons burned into your soul."

Lost, Confused, & Listening to Otis

If you ever leave me,
Leave some PCP on the dresser.
I'm gonna go crazy
When it sets in that we're not together.

Your friends don't believe
That we'll rise and succeed
Watch me change their minds,
For you, my heart bleeds.

If you ever walk away,
Just make sure you leave
Me some ibuprofen
To relieve this pain I'll be going through.
Forever you stay—that's what I'm hoping.

I know I made mad mistakes,
But baby, I wasn't focused.
Maybe if you noticed,
I've been listening to Otis
With the blues, lost and confused,
Don't know if you're coming or going.
This heartbreak got me subdued.

We may not always agree,

Or see things eye to eye,

But it's you I need

We'll be better side by side.

If you leave, make sure there's some peroxide,

So I can antisepticize

The marks where my heart died.

Maybe I was too immature,

Young and bored,

But baby, with you,

I have grown and matured.

I promised to make you happy,

To please you,

And provide you all

The essentials that you need, boo.

I'm sorry

I know you've heard this all before.

But if you really leave,

Leave some weed in the drawer.

I can't take this pain

I need to be medicated.

I'm standing in the rain,

In vain, because I hesitated.

Your college graduation
Sorry I never made it.
I was too busy being infatuated
With other women and sedated.
I'm gracious
For your loyalty and patience.
Can't believe we made it
This far, and you ain't split.

I know I ain't sh!t
I lie and connive,
Out all night chasing girls with the guys.
I apologize,
But I'll probably mess up again.
I'll stop using drugs too
I love you.

I don't want nobody else, I want just you.
You're my addiction,
You provided what I was missing.
Gave me a grip when
I was lost and slipping
I was really tripping,
Acting indifferent.

Left in the Rain

Thanks shorty, you left me in the rain,
You left me when it was pain.
When you came back
I thought things would change,
But I was lost in all the confusion
that was in my brain.
But it's all God
'cause I see where I stand, strange,
I'm going to go my separate ways,
I hope you do the same.

I was really upset when you left me,
I wanted to make things right,
But it was in your hands, you were a lefty,
Always wanted to fight.

Only thing you blessed me with
was bad karma and bills,
I know I'm in my feelings but this is how I feel,
I know it's real, had to pinch my wrist,
You broke my seal,
You unwrapped a twist.

Now I'm sipping the Chardonnay,
Wishing these paintings would go away,
Even though you say you left,
The message of what you did stayed.

I was afraid to date again,
I couldn't erase what's within,
My heart had to apologize to myself,
For the ways that I played my part in this sin.

Within five years I aged terribly,
Your ways rained terror on me.
But I'm standing here, still breathing,
Learning to let you be.

You left me in the rain,
But I found my own umbrella,
No more chasing your pain,
I'm becoming a better fella.

Thanks shorty, for the lessons learned,
For the bridges that we burned.
I'm walking my separate way now,
With the wisdom that I've earned.

Elusive dreams 2

I hate her.
I wish I could erase her.
Have another girl take the place of her.
I'm disgraced by her,
She treated me like I can't be replaced, bruh.

My face hurts from all this crying,
Lying to my friends
While she's out there flying,
Getting high in...
Had me in the lion's den,
Shoelaces tied to my shins,
Tripping, and crying again.

She played me,
Then plagued me,
Traded me for an eighth of weed.
Said she loved me
But hated me.
I wish I'd never agreed.
To proceed faithfully.

I wish my skin was tougher than leather,
But she played with my emotions.

And I let her.
She had me open
with those fake love letters,
Filled with lies,
Wrapped in disguise.
Meanwhile, she was loving another guy.
Again I start to cry.

I hate those blue eyes!
How they tell beautiful lies
Every time that she decides
To flip her vibe.

Her bipolar ways
Made me look like a fool.
Why'd you leave my heart
Drowning in blues?
B!tch, bye!

I don't ever want to see you again.
You shattered my heart down to a tenth,
Then laughed in my face.
My love turned into hate.
You were a fake,
The prettiest snake.
I treated you great.

You crushed me like a grape,
Chewed me like a piece of steak,
Spit me out like vinegar taste.
Now I'm bitter,
Can't even face my face.

Bitten by the snake
That I tried to save.
The venom's kicking,
My soul is starting to cave.

I hate that hoe.
I wish I'd known how this would go.
Now I'm feeling like an a$$hole,
Alone and vulnerable.
Lifted her high, like a flag on a pole,
Thought I could change her,
Tame her,
She harassed my soul.

I thought I could contain her.
But she's still the same her,
Same fur,
Same curse,
Same trash as before.

Threw me shade,
Made me the clown.
Now I just want to forget
She was ever around.

She burned to the ground, her bridges,
She punished me, tortured me.
Hope I learn from this sh!t.
She took a portion of me.

I should've kept my guard up.
Never thought this slut
Would give up the butt
So quick.
Now I'm stuck
With bitterness,
Pain that won't quit.
I was in love with a stripper chick,
Now I'm remorseful like a tipper gets.

When it rains, it pours,
But it won't rain riches.
Tried to take a whore
Who ain't sh!t
And make something more.
My spirit is torn now I'm sore.

I'm deflated.

That b!tch—excuse my pettiness
Never cared.
Her heart was never there.
I was used and abused
By a pretty chick
That never cared.

She hurt me, deserted me,
Left me unworthy.
Burned me, certainly.
Gave me emotional herpes
Popped up every now and then
To haunt me purposely.
We cannot be friends.

I wish I'd never met her.
Carl Thomas
Lord, I swear, if I could reset her,
I'd leave her stranded in the Bahamas.
Now she's just a wine stain
On a white tux
A permanent mark
On a love boat that once gave a f*ck

Betrayed but not Broken

Last night, I bit my tongue till it bled,
words I could've said,
but silence became the weapon instead.
I'm a real one—born thoroughbred.

You played pretend,
smiling with knives hid behind that grin,
calling me "bro,"
but plotting like an enemy from within.

Thought we was cool
turns out I was the fool.
You used me like a tool,
borrowed my loyalty,
then broke every rule.

Called me annoying,
while I was praying in the booth,
dropping verses laced with truth,
while you were out there lying too.

Pretty face, eyes locked on my gems,
but your soul got scars,
you love the spotlight

and forget who built your bars.
I never judged you,
stood tall when they clowned your name,
I took hits for you,
but you fed me the blame.

You flipped quick for somebody new,
I never played you dirty,
but you did what you do.

If I'm a fiend, then what that makes you?
'Cause I stayed ten toes
while you changed halfway through.

You called me crazy—nah, I'm just awake.
You fake deep, and I peeped the snake.
I held my peace while you spread them lies,
but karma keeps receipts,
and the truth never dies.

Now I move quiet—no talk of revenge,
I'm God's child, my glow doesn't end.
You took my love for weakness,
but that made me strong.
The real ones heal,
the fake ones move on.

You broke my heart,
but not my code.
I still pray for your peace
while I carry this load.

See, I was loyal to the core,
you were loyal to the moment.
I gave you my back,
you gave me atonement.

I'm done bleeding for folks
who clap when I fall.
I'm standing tall
betrayed, but not broken at all.

Thought we was cool,
but I was fooled.
Still I rise through the pain,
Lesson learned, wisdom gained.
You can't dim my shine with your rain
I'm a thoroughbred,
born to break every chain.

Cryonyx 2: A Second Chance

Here we go again... The second chance at this romance, but the same wretched, sorrowful ending. I guess your insecurities added to your infirmities. That only infuriated me permanently. You claimed, then blamed it on relationship PTSD. That gave you the excuse to break up with me every week, got me losing sleep over things I couldn't control while I was in this penitentiary.

But I thought that eventually, you would again trust me—especially when I'm in a cell with just me. But you came to me with accusation after accusation, adding to the already stressful situation I was facing. What you did was unjust, but I tried to adjust to the mistrust and the jealousy. My gut kept telling me that she's probably just making an excuse to bail and leave. Ironically, I never thought that you'd abuse me, accuse me, then use me for motivation. But in hindsight, I saw those ulterior motives waiting. When I was in jail, quarantined, you stayed away from me—but it wasn't my fault, I was in a cell and couldn't leave. I know I couldn't call at all, but in your mind, I was fine, calling another whore. Then, when you picked up the phone, you wouldn't press four. You just let it ring while I was being ignored. My heart was tormented, my eyes were pouring. It started storming--to Cryonyx. Oh, not again—my so-called lover and best friend, whom a lot of my time and my money I invested in. Damn, you even sent me an email that was meant for him!

Then all of a sudden, you just wanted to be friends in the prime of cuffing season--for no fucking reason. Or maybe it is for a fucking reason. Now I'm fucked up, bleeding, a week before Christmas—I meant Xmas. You melted my heart like a marshmallow, Swiss Miss. This chick flipped for a quick hit, left me in jail with no breakfast, and I felt desperate; I felt like my head split.

The black tears are looking familiar. It's always the closest ones to you that will hurt you and kill ya, then break you down and pretend to build you up. This can't be real love; remorse is build-up. You didn't even give me the decency of explaining this to me instead of texting me, then deleting me. That was a cowardly move, especially to a guy who buys flowers and empowers you. Why are you all of a sudden acting sour, boo?

It's like I'm limited to what I'm allowed to do, but you still think I have other women? How are you going to go off of intuition that is probable? You suddenly leave me for no reason during the holiday season, which made me hungry, watching other people eating. I'm not cheating; you're not seeing the big picture, just thinking about yourself and controlling expenditures and fixtures.

You were supposed to be my elixir. When I was down, you were supposed to pick me up, but you kicked me to the curb in a way that was absurd. Then you had the nerve to tell me it was my idea first? Huh, I don't see it. I was acquitted of all of your charges. It's just bullshit—those mute excuses that your anxiety was wicked. That's why your appearances kept going missing. You would lie to me, saying your phone isn't in a position for you to get it.

Ex-ploding

Wow—I really thought you were the one I loved.
But instead, you left me with a dud.
You lied to me— game is all you supplied me.
You got what you wanted, then you cut ties to me.

Deceitfully, you saw me as a place to stay.
Confusing and subduing me, straight to my face.
You used your looks to hook me
in your web of deceit.
Had me tripping and weak,
tangled and de-feeted—literally.

I should've seen it coming;
your words were redundant.
You had me dumbing, crying—like an onion.
took me to dinner so my pockets could break fast.
You left me hungry while I was lunching.

The only meal you wanted was a mil.
But not all money is legal, as it appeals
I was out here working, making an honest living.
I never knew you'd do me like Mike

playing Robin Givens.

What you weren't robbing; I was giving.

I was so mindlessly generous.

Just to fit your benefits.

I should've peeped the bitterness

and the vindictiveness.

When my sister mentioned this.

Despite all that, you still played Miss Innocent.

I should have ended it.

But I was too invested in this relationship.

Now I feel contested and congested.

complacentness led to laziness.

Now I'm sitting here,

Feeling like Boo Boo the Fool

Sulking on this bar stool.

On how I was used and abused.

Indulging, as induced by Johnnie Walker.

While my heart... ex-plodes. 💔

I'm off ya!

I wanna throw you in the commode!

Crash course

Yeah, it's as bad as it seems
I'm an emotional wreckage meme,
crashed out from the last bad dream
That replayed like a crime scene.

Maybe I should breeze?
She tried to cover her venereal faults with Febreze.
She thought she was giving me Mac n cheese.
But she really was sexually assaulting me,

Looking for purpose
In the aftermath of the crash,
thought she was good on the surface,
But masks crack fast.

Is it my fault
that I wear my thoughts on my sleeves?
With no support, I was caught,
Now I'm grieving what I believed.

She tried to hide her damage
with perfume and pretty words,
sold me comfort in disguise,
But her comfort hurt.

We were boxed in
toxic, locked in,
fighting, crying, then leave again.
Verbal jabs like we were boxing
No time to bob or weave the pain.

We should've left,
But we were fiends for the fix,
addicted to the chaos,

mistaking it for bliss.

Forgiveness turned into remission,
a plea bargain with pain
We kept circling the same frame.
Nobody innocent,
Nobody wins,
Only disaster waiting to begin.

Why start a love
When you've no plan to finish it?
We argued, broke up,
then made up,
Then I woke up in the same storm again.
This was so obnoxiously toxic
a monotonous loop of opposites
attracting the opposition.
And now I'm standing in the wreckage,
finally saying what we wouldn't admit:

We gotta stop this.
We gotta stop this.
We gotta stop this.

Chapter 3: Flesh and Fire

The passion, the lust, the temptation — love through the body before the soul.

"Desire leads, the body speaks before the heart. Lust, temptation, and the blaze of fleeting connection might make you fall apart. That fire that burns fast, leaves marks, and forces growth."

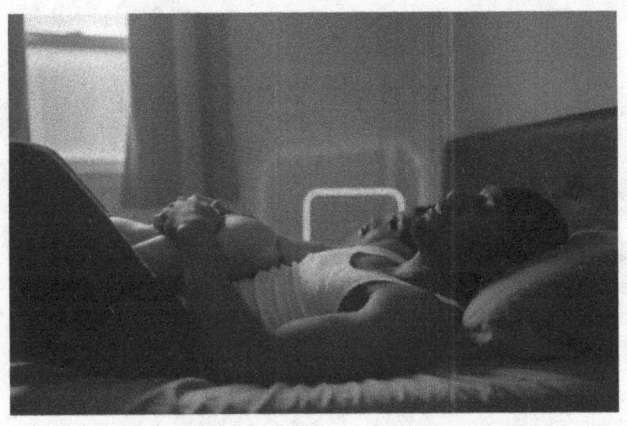

Flesh Without Fire

What was that
your breath on mine,
our bodies locked,
but hearts misaligned.

Chest to chest,
thigh to thigh,
yet your gaze
looked past the sky.

You moved like silk,
but I felt the lie
your moans were hollow,
your heat ran dry.

The rhythm missed,
the spark fell flat,
I kissed your lips
but tasted lack.

I wasn't there
not really, no.
You'd given your yes
to another show.

So I played my part,
but not my soul.
You had my flesh,
but not control.

Now I lie still,
numb from the try
sex without spirit,
a ghosted high.

Microwave love

I. Confession

I'm sorry, but this is how I feel.

If you want me to go slow, then for you

and only you—I will.

I don't care whether we go out or whether we chill.

I just want to be around you,

because when I'm with you,

it feels like time stands still.

You give me instant gratification that's accountable.

But I'm sorry for being an a$$hole

and a little bit too emotional.

II. Fantasy & Faith

I had it all figured out

how this was supposed to go:

You would be my queen,

I would be your superhero.

I would be king—master

and we'd be together, living happily ever after.

I guess that's just a Cinderella dream,

or a storied scene from a fairytale.

Because when it comes to this dating thing,

I don't seem to fit or fare well.

III. Self-Awareness

I always end up giving all of me way too soon.

I know I need to give you room

to let our flowers bloom.

You're mine, baby—you just don't know it.

I know you feel me too;

you didn't say it,

but you showed it.

We'll grow if

it's written in the planets and stars,

but I'm going to let it flow,

and keep the door ajar.

IV. Temptation & Humor

I can't wait for the next text from you

that's a moment closer to being next to you.

Lettuce, like a vegetable, get sexual,

then I'll let you know that

I'm extraordinarily exceptional.

Hopefully, I'm patient,

because I'm terrible at waiting.

I know you can hear the anticipation

in our conversations.

V. Drive & Determination

Right now I gotta go

got power moves to make and cheese to chase,

so I can break fast, my wins.

But you're eggsactly who I need

to break bread with in the end.

You give me inspiration to bring home that bacon.

I want to be more than a friend.

I hope to see you sooner than later

maybe in the back of a Maybach Benz;

it depends.

VI. Waiting & Wanting

If you're free, call me instantly,

so we can discuss our point of view

through a unique vantage lens.

Until then,

I'll be waiting impatiently

for your phone call,

to set up a sneaky link with a grin.

I can't wait for the next time we speak again

or meat again.

I'm going to think about you

every second of the hour,

because I'm weak again.

VII. Yearning & Reverence

You give me that power

to devour my stresses.

Yes, miss—you're a ten.

Your presence is the only medicine

that can soothe me.

So until you hit me up,

I'ma be watching love movies on Tubi,

sweating you profusely to come and do me.

Groovy.

VIII. Plea

Don't confuse me,

or lead me on,

or leave me on read.

I want you right now.

Helllooo...

helllooo...

hellloooooo...

You heard what I said?

Don't make me double text — you know I mean every

word I bled.?

Frozen Desire

She whispered rivers, gold, and flame,
A sultry vow that made me ache.
Her tongue traced promises in my name.
A prayer she'd moan for pleasure's sake.

But all she gave was a heatless game,
Her body close, her hunger faked.
She teased with fingers, lips that came.
So near the edge I'd almost break.

I chased the breath she moaned, then hid,
Through sheets of snow and primal need.

She spread her thighs, then closed—forbid
The very thing that made me plead.

Each kiss she gave, a frozen twist,
Her wetness promised, but was never shown.
I tasted nothing on my lips but mist.
A chance denied, my seed unsown.

Her name was winter wrapped in lace,
Black silk that barely hid her curves.
I traced her thighs, her secret place.
She stayed unmoved despite my fervent nerves.

She lit no fire in our embrace,
Just frost where passion once had burned.
Her nipples were hard, but not from grace
Just a cold refusal, and a lesson learned.

She arched like dawn, her back a bow,
Then it turned to dusk before I came.
A touch that swelled me, made me grow,
But never let me play with her thang.

I craved her warmth, her scent, her taste,
The grip of her around my BBC.
But she was ice beneath the waist,

A tease who'd never let me feed.

Her moans were theater, skillfully done,
Her grinding hips are a practiced art.
She'd stroke until I almost won,
Then leave me hard, aching, torn apart.

So now I lie where heat once stirred,
My shaft is still thick with want and nill.
She promised ecstasy in every word.
Flesh on flesh, the ultimate thrill.

But all I got was empty space,
Blue-balled and burning in the cold.
She wore desire with pretty lace,
But never let the story be told.

A sexy angel dressed in sin,
Who swore she'd ride me through the nightfall.
Instead, she left me locked within.
This prison of her teasing is spiteful.

I braved the storm for cheeks and thighs,
For legs wrapped tight and breathy screams.
But she just whispered pretty lies.
And left me choking on my dreams.

Survived the Fire

wake to the quiet now,

not the chaos of yesterday,

But the whisper of lessons learned today

The echo of mistakes that shaped me.

The streets that once swallowed me

raised me...

now feel distant,

like a nightmare I survived

but still carried in my chest, while I'm living.

I see my reflection differently today.

Not perfect, not whole,

But in an honest way.

Every scar, every bruise, every wrong turn

has been a teacher,

even when I refused to learn.

I kneel without shame,

not asking for a pass

But for guidance.
God listens, even when I fail,
even when my own hands
push me back into the silence.

I feel the weight of my choices,
the ones that built walls, burned bridges,
and left my heart in isolation.
Yet there is light
in knowing I survived the fire.
I was attacked in phases.

That survival is not a permission slip
to return to my old ways,
But a call to rise higher than my old days.

The mirrors I once avoided
I face it now with clarity.
I see a man who wrestled with himself,
and sometimes lost,
But who is learning to stand without charity.

The days of chasing illusions
of wealth, pleasure, and false security

faded into memory.
I am learning to seek truth,
to value myself beyond the moment,
to protect my body, mind, and soul.
And use God's remedies.

I walk through this life carefully,
not afraid of the pain that shaped me,
But aware that it can guide me
If I let it.

I am no longer my worst enemy,
Though the battle continues.
I am a work in progress,
a story still being written,
a reflection being mended

One day at a time.

Hula Hoops

Why do I have to jump through all these hula hoops
Just to prove to you that I want to be with you?
Why do I have to show and prove
the truth for you to,
still overlook what's really real and how I really feel,
To get through your skepticism?
These texts that I typed for you
actually have messages in them.

I just want to be more than just friends.

Why do you have so much suspense
When are our conversations intense?
Relating our events
to past relationships are offensive.
I'm not him, sis—I'm offended
By constantly having to be defensive,
Defending men that I don't even know
that you're mentioning.

Then when things get intensive,
You'd rather sit on the fences
Instead of commenting on them
like we've recommended.
I'm just trying to get to know you on another level
That is sufficient for us to be really in a relationship.

It doesn't take common sense to add up
The additions and inflictions
That have influenced you to listen
To what you want subconsciously, inconveniently
Trying to convey to me.
What are you trying to say to me?
Lately I've been staring in the mirror...
slowly picking my heart apart.

Burning thru the furnace

Could this be that this was meant to be?
That's the only way this makes sense to me.
I knew one day you'd come to me eventually
It was evident that you were sent to me,
Inevitable for you to come to me.
I knew once you seen me, the rest would be history.
I ain't no mystery, I'm a king fit for a queen.
I'm young, hung, and handsome,
we make a good team.
I'll be the calm to your stormy weather,
I'll do whatever it takes to make you better.
I'll step up when you're doing bad, would never let ya
I see you as a jewel in a lost treasure.
I'm glad that I found you, I hope that it's forever.
Whether we're together or not, I'll go the extra measures
To communicate with you through emails and letters.
I see the great in you, plus you're beautiful and better.
At least to me you're cute and suitable.
I'm going to make love to you
from your head to your cuticles.
I knew just exactly what to do to you
To make you come back to me, satisfactory, ooh.
But I really want to get through your mental
And know everything that you've ever been through

Before I ever lay this 9+ inches in your physical
I want our connection to be spiritual.
I knew when I first heard you, I was feeling you.
You have this down-to-earth, sexy appeal in you.
RIP to your ex, dude—you knew I had to steal you
When I seen the down chick and the real in you.

And hopefully when you leave, you'll still be true.
Keep in touch with me, I'll be home soon in June.
You got me attracted like metal to a magnet,
And you don't have to be the baddest bad chick
All I need you to be is down, loyal, and average.
Your voice helps me get through this madness.
Your soul is beautiful, that's a fact, miss.
I just want to introduce you to this passion.
You sound so cute when you're laughing.
You may not be used to this romantic brashness
Or tactfulness—this isn't by an accident.
Us meeting each other, you were asking for him,
But I know you needed me is what I was imagining.
They say there's a reason for everything that happens.
I hope you're here for more than a season
I'd be mad and sick.
I want to build something real and everlasting
That can go through the furnace
and won't melt like plastic.

Heaven-Sent and Hell-Bent

I'm going to give you a pass, miss
You stood me up on our first date.
I was going through something, wishing
This could be some kind of passion escape

From the life I'm living in,
Full of sin I didn't want you in.
But that was a mistake.
I thought this night would be without a hitch,
Didn't see the snares, the glitch.

This could've been elation
Instead of thoughts of carnal penetration
Using me against myself,
Taking tolls on my health.
I just thought this night would help.

I felt... a real glimpse of heaven
As I stared dead into your eyes,
Hoping I'd see the skies
Drop atomic bombs of pleasure,
Bless me with your chest of treasures.

Yes, I guess I overstepped my boundaries,
Speaking profoundly like I just seen
The sweetest cutie pie
With a pair of grey-blue eyes.
Knew for sure you'd join the team

I'd never second-guess
A present from heaven sent.
As I looked into your eyes, reeling you in,
Hoping this wasn't the last time
I'd see your pretty face in this place.
But as I wait for your answer
Like a Cancer would do for you
Holla at me, boo, if you think this is true.
And if it's about you, then it is what it is,
And it will be what it be
Until infinity.

Chapter 4: Ghosted by Love

Absence, distance, and the ache of being unseen.+

"When love disappears, silence fills the space. This chapter explores being left behind, feeling invisible, and learning that absence can teach as much as its presence make."

Hollow Gestures

I find myself at a loss for words,
Standing in the wreckage of what we were.
Your actions, steeped in disrespect and abuse,
Have left their mark upon my soul like a noose.
A lasting impact that I cannot undo.
Was it all justifiable to you?

Did you sleep soundly while I was breaking apart?
I believed that you had my best interests at heart,
That your hands would hold, not harm me,
That your voice would heal, not cut me.

Yet your toxic ways seeped into my path.
Like poison leaking through cracked glass,
Slow and certain, spreading through
Every breath, Every thought about you

I tried to convince myself this was love.
What you offered turned into what you dubbed
Promises became weapons,
Care became control,
Support became suffocation.

The transformation was so gradual

I didn't see it until I was drowning.
Your hollow gestures mirrored my mental downing.
Empty words echoing in empty rooms,
A relentless onslaught chipping away left wounds

In my well-being, my sense of self,
At everything I thought I knew.
Not tending to my health
I am learning now to name what happened:
This was not love.
This was not a partnership.
This was not what I deserved.
Your inaction.

And though you left me fractured,
I am still here.
Still standing.
Still finding my words again.
The impact you left are lasting,
But so am I.
Now I'm fasting!!!

Cold call

Pick up the phone
Pick up the phone!
Are you too busy to speak to me?
Is there someone else in your home,
Or are you on the creep?
I just wanted to talk to you for a few minutes,
Then you can go back to sleep
Or whatever you was doing when we finished.
When I was spending,
you didn't have a problem with my ways,
But now that I'm in prison,

You're spinning me like I'm some waves.

But when I was home,
You used to have me hostage on the phone.
Now all of a sudden there's times
When you claim you don't got your phone.
But you answer it when it is convenient,
Or when you needing free rent
Then you answer me quick.
You don't think I see this shit.

How are you even asking me for cash when I'm in jail?
You must think I'm a trick, I can tell,
But that ship has been sailed.
I'm in here fighting for my life,
Where most would tell,

But instead I'm getting solicited
Entitlement stipends from my wife.
And the only other time you would answer my calls
Is when you were not being crazy,
Romantically enthralled.
You're wrong!

but I still loved you,
But now I hate you

Because you couldn't even stay faithful.
I would've waited forever and a day for you,

But you left me to fight the United racist States,
Striped and stripped of my rights.
You were supposed to be my wife,
But you decided to skate.
I beat life in the state,
But now I'm in a place
where the feds got a 98% conviction rate,
With 20 years over my head
It's hard to live in this fate.

Suicide was in the back of my mind,
But I had to swallow my pride and man up
If I had to do the time.
I would be fine
As long as I have you by my side
You're my superpowers and my kryptonite
At the same time.

Now I'm in a place of darkness,
I need someone to talk with,
But you won't pick up the phone,
Left me alone,
Which was heartless.

A love/hate Dance

Every interaction
was tainted by conflict,
each word was a spark
in the dry grass of our silence.
You filled the air,
suffocating my space,
stifling the small,
trembling voice that sought to erase.
Compliments tossed like coins
into an empty well,
only to be retrieved
before they could echo—failed.
denying me even

the shimmer of worth
I tried to believe was mine.
You treated me like dirt

You loomed large,
a shadow swallowing light,
a presence too heavy to draw
parasitic, patient,
feeding on my flaws
beneath the hush of night.
We moved in circles,
a dance of love and hate,
clinging and breaking,
hurting and healing our faith
Our rhythm is forever off-beat.
This was not the song I had envisioned,
not the tenderness I dreamed.
Yet still,
beneath the aches,
A quiet strength stirred my faith
a pulse whispering:
I was meant to be more
than the silence you left behind.
I am great!

Duck Duck Goose

I thought you would be loyal—that's how it felt—but you sure turned out to be spoiled like milk. The whole time, your game was as smooth as silk, but you turned out to be just polyester and a messed-up MILF. If all you planned to do was screw when you pursued me, couldn't you have told me unruly? We could have moved in that direction, but I wanted to give you the benefit of the doubt, to see what you were about. But your actions don't match the words coming out of your mouth. My intuition was trying to warn me, but I ignored it. It sensed that you were trying to get whatever you could get.

Whatever you were after, you got it out of me. Obviously, I was just a trick, a win from the lottery. Nah! I don't need your apology. You lied to me, and now we can't ever be friends. Don't say hi to me. Don't even say my name—just say bye to me. You betrayed my trust just to get high? Why? Wasn't it enough to just have your addiction supplied? I should've known I couldn't compete with drugs. You proved to be incomplete to me—a dub. You saw the best of me. You had the best palm in West Palm, but you were just sand on the beach. I was warned!! You tried to make me bawl till I fall too, but I landed on my feet. I won't be in the field running around with my cleats. Don't be quick to open your mouth to eat every time I get my cheese. I can't live with it. Don't act like Oscar the Grouch with me.

Say thanks for the gifts I bestowed upon you out of God's grace. Instead, you looked in my face like a trick—your highness—intending to take advantage of my hospitality and kindness. Maybe I had temporary blindness to the fact that I gave you the benefit to show tenderness. So when I play the same game better, there shouldn't be any bitterness. Never forget this. Now you have to live with it. And don't try to act all naive and innocent. You knew what you did to set up this predicament. It's ridiculous, this childish act you tried to run on me just to get one up on me. But now you're done to me. It's nothing for me to bounce back and get on the grind. I'd rather have wasted my money before I wasted my time.

Funny thing is, I saw that goose egg you tried to lay, but I ducked ducked it and got smooth out the way. You tried to sell something that was nothing. You said you had a bun in the oven and that it was mine, but it wasn't. I didn't flinch. I ain't bragging, but I mostly saw lies, and the other stuff? I used the magnums. But now you're trying to charge me like a Dodge, but I dodge it like Tommy Lasorda. You tried to set a court order to take out a quarter from me. Our paternity test is most certainly 98% sure it wasn't me... why i outta!!! no honeymooning.

I already saw you were calculating to purchase off me. You were just a user, unworthy of me. You tried to pull me down to the ground personally. You knew I was generous and spent my chips on family and friends and looked out for the kids. I thought you had potential, but you only wanted instant revenue. So you threw all your morals and principles out the window. I thought you'd be a better you, but the second you got a better view of my cheddar, you ended the relationship.

Family Tithes

It does seem like the ones that were the closest to me did the most to me. When everything was all Gucci, it was all rosy like it was supposed to be. But when the tears dropped from the skies and the heavens used to cry, I would still feel the pain from their reins in my life. That was abusive, a wry high that strained and stained my brain so deep it dyed me numb. They tried to come for me, and I still don't know why or where from. They were bad company, and I can't deny that. I remember every grimy family member who did me dirty. It's all measured in my life. I almost died.

As the ice melted in my veins, the things they did to me stopped hurting, 'cause it all became in vain. Then I started to take the pain. People claimed they would change, but their actions stayed the same. It's a shame—they were just gaming me, trying to gain some change, thinking I was rich like Dana Dane with fame. Scheming on my chips, and my dumb a$$ kept letting my guard down like a hobo clown, just to have them around once again, on a whim, they put chips on my golden crown. I wasn't wise enough, so I'd frown. Then it was crickets when they'd bounce, like a bad check out of town.

They robbed and stole from me, but never kept it real—only chilled with me 'cause of my clout. Nevertheless, in any amount, if they could've gotten away with my dollar bills, they probably would've killed me without a doubt. So I had to keep it real with myself — open my eyes and shut my mouth. I gave them the rope and let them choose their route. I still trusted them, 'cause I still had love for them, when I should've dubbed them—cut them off, cut them out. Should've flushed them down the drain. Now I'm surrounded by disdain. They were supposed to be my family, my loved ones, but they loved to give me pain.

They even tried to steal my cash—word! Got into my accounts and changed the passwords. It was just my birthday, but backwards. What an a$$ I was, 'cause only they could've known that information. The crazy part? I only found out from the hazardous notifications. They even tried to transfer my funds to a Western Union location, but my credit union wasn't stupid — they knew exactly what they were doing. Now they ruined my trust and funds again. I can't even trust my funds with my friends or my family, obviously. There's always gonna be this suspense that they're after me. I'm not paranoid, nor is it anxiety—this is just the aftermath of a real tragedy of what really happened to me, not a parody. I didn't choose my family; they just happened to be related by blood but correlated inaccurately. They didn't fare to care for half of me. Sadly, family ain't family no more, especially if you're poor—'cause the rich got us in an expensive figure-four revolving door war.

Unfortunately, I'm tied to my family tree where fortune bleeds greed, envy, and insanity. But being the man that I be, Imma ride or die with them—it's F.O.E. until eternity. You heard me 😁

 (heartfist)

I just had to thank God directly for protecting me

From your grimy, nasty, inconsiderate a$$

for not infecting me,

Respectfully.

And for me, being not affectingly...

Caught up in your web of deceit

Your ways of cheating on me

Recently and regularly.

You are full of bullsh!t, miss.

Butt thank God I missed those bullets

that were recklessly

Sprayed out of your full clip.

You were sent by the devil to wreck me

You had only one goal...

To have me dig my own grave with your shovel

And have my ways disheveled.

You tricked me to get d!ck from me

on various levels.

Gassing me up like a pedal,

But when the problems arose,

You were just a thorn with no petals.

I'm sorry, but I'm not sorry
that I dodged your quicksand, witch!
You knew that I was Muslim.
You were still trying to hand-feed me
ham sandwiches b!tch!

You were trying to get me to eat diseases
right out of your bosom.
I had to act like I was asleep to play possum,
But I don't eat dead red meat.

No thanks to that voodoo pudding.
You tried to have my wood in
like a spoon in your dish.
You had me like I was Dr. Phil-feel Gooden,
But now I'm pitching no-hitters.
I quit her, then dissed her,
then flipped the script on her.
Then put so much distance between her
That she just became a nonexistent blur.

That no good, sick, loose goose chick.

Tried to spruce a noose on my brute boot,
which is ludicrous.
Get out of my way, move b!tch!!!
Whew... Thank you so much, Lord,
For protecting my long sword.
Knowing that I was only with her
Because I was vulnerable and bored.
But now I ignore all her calls.

Jezebel spells almost had me fell into a deep well.
Being a lost cause and overboard.
Into the triple stages of darkness.
For she was infectious, vicious, and heartless.
I don't want any parts of it,
So can y'all pardon my riffs.
She tried to put my heart in her fist.
But thank God that I dodged that sh!t....
What a heartless b!tch!!!

I Thought We Were Cool

Last night, you had me uptight.
It took all of my might
not to start a verbal fight.

I've never been a hater all my life,
so for you to talk slick behind my back wasn't right.
I thought we were cool
but I was fooled.
Guess I was just being used
for what you needed me to do.
Just because you're beautiful
doesn't mean you're thorough.
I'm from the boroughs,
where we gotta earn respect and dinero.

All I expected was
you wouldn't be a weirdo,
calling me annoying
while I'm sending your letters here, though.
And your man is my bro
So how does that go?

But I didn't say shit;
kept my mouth zipped,
even when you flipped,
then dissed me

for a person you just met
you got me vexed, B.
If I'm a whore's son,
Does that make you wholesome?
I ain't judging, I'm just troublesome.
You were my girl's friend
I thought I could trust one.
You looked official,
like a whistle—what's up with you, hun?

Even when Rock dissed you,
I never dismissed you.
I stood up for you
That's why he switched his tune.

I thought we were cool
but I was fooled.
You took my kindness as weakness,
so cruel.
But I don't hold grudges,
don't play the fool.
Won't throw your name in mud
that ain't the move.

I'll accept your flaws with love,
That's the truth.
I'm a sure bet—no need to prove.
If I eat, my people eat.

We all succeed,
stand on our own two feet.
I ain't never been greedy.
When my friends are needy,
I'm there—believe me.

I thought we were cool
but I was fooled.
If I did things that annoyed you,
why not tell me,
instead of another dude
Who's annoying too?

I don't hate you,
I won't diss you.
I'd rather uplift you,
help and assist you.
I might be extra,
but I keep it real with my issues.
So why throw shade on me
for someone new
Who disrespects you?
I thought we were cool
but I was fooled.
Still keeping it real,
never fake
even when loyalty's at stake.
Loyalty's easy to speak, but hard to live.

Love skitzo

When it comes to love with us, it's a dub miss
You've broken the trust ships.
Now there are issues and glitches in this system,
a selfish, one-sided relationship,
a suicidal self-destruction mission
And I'm not with it.

I should've known from the start
when you were vague with your ways.
When I saw us start to fall apart,
I stayed, to my dismay.
I didn't pay attention,
and now I'm getting
all these expensive consequences,
coming in repetitive sequences.
This isn't legit.
You said you were a real one,
But all I'm getting is counterfeits.

I'm living off Ritalin
My nutritionist says I'm vitamin-U deficient,
suffering this extended, intensive, bedridden infliction
of love addiction.
There's no way of fixing it.

Your maleficent disrespect still has after-effects.
I'm affected by its illicit emissions.
After the lust was gone,
So was its effect.
Now I regret ever kissing your neck.

The time I lost
I couldn't afford those hits on my checks.
The hate escalated; I missed those steps.
I was tripping, big shoes,
thinking you were different
standing to be corrected in my views.
I didn't listen to my inner strength,
my intuition.
I confess...
I was skitzing when I was vexed,
crazy, bugged, drugged,
had no self-respect
I was lost in confusion.
A sucker for your painful bruising,
amazingly in love—foolish.
Stupid Cupid shot me.
With his naked gun—no OJ.
I'm taking off the gloves.
No more play.
I'm done.

You can't come run it back.

I was loyal to a fault,

but your love wasn't attached.

I had yours,

but you had a gun to my back

and a knife to my throat.

I was always under your attacks;

My life was your hoax.

You were supposed to be my wife

But nope.

To you, my life was a joke.

You were nice when you spoke,

But that was just all smoke

a mask that you carried,

You went from Mariah to Jim Carrey.

Scary. I couldn't cope.

You never cared for me,

only carried me

there when you were in need.

You played your part with glee.

Barely there for me when I needed you,

and I was too feeble to believe it was true.

Deceitful, evil,

And I was too blind in love

to see it in you.

The lies, the disrespect

I had to check myself
before I wrecked my health.
You had my neck in your belt,
My check was your wealth.
I guess I needed help.
I thought that was the love that I felt.

I was working while you were purring,
looking perfect,
made me a pick-'em victim
of your generational curses.
Worthless.
A hermit.
While you turned into Miss Piggy,
I was your Kermit,
determined not to be your rotisserie.
Hurting, blurting profanities
to the psychological surgeons
operating on my broken heart and kidneys.
While you were with me,
You played with my emotions like a Frisbee,
channeling my buttons for entertainment, Disney.
I tried therapeutic conversions,
But it was purposeless.
I wasted so much time.
My biological clock almost stopped working.

I was the one you didn't accept
except when I made your purchases.
I don't deserve this ish
I swear to God, I swore to God,
blaming Him for my imperfections.
This isn't fair—this is hard,
harder than a Pinocchio erection.
Still, you showed me no affection.
I didn't see your perception
of my projections from afar.
I was far off,
thought it was all my fault,
that I could make it up
with all the stuff I bought.
But that came to naught.
Now I'm caught, cuffed in court,
stuck in my thoughts,
wishing I'd made better decisions
before being hauled off to New York
for trumped-up reports.
They're trying to send me up north,
turn my mind to a corpse
with indictments.
I don't know if I'll see my wife again.
Even through the trifling events,
I'd still like her in my life

as a friend.

Crazy, right?
This fight never ends.
Twice last night
I tried to slice my wrist.
Now I'm trying to keep it cool,
even though she put me through hell
where ice doesn't exist.

How can she be so cruel?
But it is what it is.
I'll be with her when I get out
because I love what I love,
and without her,
I can't be without.
No doubt
She still thinks about me.
Undoubtedly, she'll never forget me.
If they ever ask her about me.

Hopefully, I'll get out of this hostile hospital
that shows no mercy or hospitality,
So I can see my baby girl one last time
Maybe she'll accept my apologies.

End Zone Dreams

When she first met me, she kept me in the friend zone,
but I was hopeful that one day I'd get into her end zone.
I don't know if she was misleading me
or feeding me the wrong signals.

She would never pledge her allegiance to me,
which came as inconceivable.
She claimed that my past was a red flag,
that she didn't know if she could believe in me
even though I was giving her all that I had so easily.

The longer she rejected me, the stronger it affected me.
Let's be real, I didn't even know if she respected me,
but I wasn't going to fall asleep behind the wheel.

She gave me her number,
but she never answered her cell;
It went straight to voicemail.
I had no other choice but to inhale,
then exhale.

I transferred that energy into me,
I still sent her messages at least once a week.
She would leave it on read.

I figured that sooner or later
she would recognize who I be,
And whoever she's with now should breeze
immediately.

I may not be the one she wants,
but I am the man that she needs.
I can get her over the hump
that I can guarantee.

But how naive of me
to think that she would change eventually.
I thought we were meant to be,
but she had other options I did not see.
I could see past her beauty.
Like Ali, she floated like a butterfly
But her lullabies stung like a bee.

I would shrug off her put-offs
and vow to turn her disavowal
into an affirmative.
I wasn't only persistent;
I was also determined.

My determination was to make it through to her mind,
which was permeated with man-hatred,

instead of with mine.
Maybe my expectations were too high,
or maybe I denied the truth and the lies.

Maybe she genuinely
didn't want to be with me.
I didn't get any bad vibes,
But just like honey attracts fruit flies,
She attracted rude guys.

In contrast, I was way different.
Maybe she couldn't see the differences
or the significance.
But who I was
was someone who was very interested,
who was also available,
who actually wanted a relationship,
was ready to commit and invest in it.

I valued her.
I empowered her.
I didn't want to settle with friends with benefits.
I would have loved her with all my strength
and would have never abandoned the ship.
But she chose to travel a different road.
God bless her soul.

Chapter 5: Love's Illusions

Deceptive affection, false connections, and lessons learned the hard way.

"Not every shine is gold. Mistaken signals, half-truths, and false intimacy live here... The mirror of love's trickery and the bitter taste of lessons learned too late isn't clear."

I dunno

I hope I won't be single for the rest of my life.
I think I'm ready to mingle,
But I really need to invest in a wife.
When it comes to dating,
It seems like every girl I meet ain't my type.
They might look good,
But their personality or priorities ain't right.
I always find something wrong…
But maybe it's me. I like what I like.
Maybe my expectations are just too high,
And the fact that my heart's a big block of ice
That just attracts fruit flies.

Or maybe it's like they say — I'm retarded,
'Cause I always nonchalantly decline.
The unsolicited advice I'm bombarded with.
I'm cold-blooded and cold-hearted,
So I take their two cents, like a grain of rice.
But it never satisfies my appetite.

These women judge me like Judy,
With their fake booties, lashes, hair, purses, nails,
Personalities, and boobies.

Still, maybe it's me.
Maybe I don't fit their traditional man prototype.

But I feel the same way when their photo hype
ain't right.
It must've been a Phypo — a photo typo,
A picture mistype.
I feel like I get tricked when they flip the switch,
'Cause the photogenic don't match the physics
Or maybe we're both right.
I dunno.

They act like they need me to pay their bills,
So I say farewell and let welfare feed 'em krills.
I'd rather be a simp than a shrimp trick
But somehow I still get conned.
Like Edison paying a light bill.
I dunno.

It's either I like them and they don't like me,
Or vice versa — more than likely.
Sometimes they wanna fight me,
Sometimes they just wanna get piped by me.
I dunno.

Maybe they took my text out of context,
Reading what I said literally
Instead of conceptually
Understanding my intent intentionally
The dating games are so strange these days.
I'd go crazy trying to figure it out,

So I just stay in my lane.

But for some strange reason,

I keep making the same mistakes.

With choices, I ain't forced to take it.

I'm emotionally insane,

Spinning in a revolving door of hate and pain

It's too hard to figure it all out.

It just leads to shouts and bouts,

Passive-aggressive words flying out our mouths.

I dunno.

Maybe I'm addicted to pain,

To decisions, I ain't forced to make.

At this state's divorce rate,

It's better to have love that's a loss.

Then being lost in a love that I hate.

I dunno.

Loneliness feels like an emotional corpse,

A dud—a scud missile missing its target.

It hurts so good to fall in love with somebody else,

Especially if they love you back.

That's what love does

Janet Jackson even said that, facts.

I dunno.

The sun shines on the earth,

The earth orbits its path,
And together they create life movement,
Something Norbit and Rasputia ain't have.
How you doin'???
I dunno.

Maybe my heart's attached to my brain,
And it doesn't match my emotional mindframe.
That's why I end up in pain,
Suffering broken-heart attacks
With ice in my veins.
I have to change.
Start over from scratch.
That ain't a chain
Making the marks on my back
I'm love, pistol-whipped.
The partners I end up with are mismatched.
My goals and relationships on the wrong track
Going nowhere fast on an emo treadmill,
Collapsing dead still.
I dunno.

Maybe that's just part of my habitat,
A habit where I'm at
Seeing my parents scrap,
Then leave for four weeks,
Then come right back.
So maybe I'm weak, in fact,

I dunno.

Because I keep returning to the cheese
Like rats to the traps.
Love got me blinded and bonded by its wrath.
That's why I keep coming back,
Time after time, with my mind off track,
But thank God He heals me when I get smacked.
But it's strange
I still never learn.
I'd have seven burns,
And by the eighth turn
I'd still be in debt to the yearn.
My only concern
Is finding that love I've missed since infancy.
Even then, I probably wouldn't listen.
With efficiency
I dunno.

Maybe I need to pay attention.
To my therapist's clenched teeth of conviction
Every time he gives advice in our sessions.
I can see his tension.
As I recount every incident
Same story, different faces.
It's ridiculous.
I dunno 🤷

I dunno what it is.

One day, I'm gonna find myself a real love
to ease the flames.
That's my aim.
I've been suffering from this burning rain
that keeps pouring into my heart and brain
feels like an everlasting explosion of emotions
I'm hoping to sustain.
Maybe I won't be just another sucker4pain,
feeling like ice was stuffed in my veins.
I might need a change. (I dunno.)
But until then, I'll puff on this Mary Jane
in my Sean John while she's in her Vera Wang,
and play with my thing.

The way she came is the way she left
fast, promising, roseate, uncompromising
an uneven exchange.
I can't take this.
Too many disappointments,
letdowns, and shoulders full of burdens
that need adjoining.
I feel like I've been anointed
with satanic ointments
facing the love courts of heaven
When my lawyer was Lucifer-appointed.
Bridges burning. Threads unstitching.

My purpose is escaping.
Missing counseling appointments
I must be on a love-suicidal mission,
collision, conversion. (I dunno.)

They say a house isn't a home
When the love is withdrawn.
Nights like this, I wish raindrops would *fallllll!*
Irregular heartbeats,
high blood pressure,
diabetes from Coca-Cola sodas
and fast-food fries with all the extras.
I'm stressed. I messed up.

Smoking cancer sticks in denial
telling myself it's not cancerous
as I smoke 'n' joke, tryna be a fashionista
but I think I need to throw in the towel. (I dunno.)

Then again, I'm spending bands on kicks,
dressing like a mannequin,
tryna be the man again
'cause I got issues of abandonment.
My life is in mismanagement.
The plan was to get a wifey
But that doesn't seem likely,
'cause I keep falling in love
with mirage mirror images

That looks just like me.
The female version of me,
acting like she's a virgin to me,
saying all the right things purposely,
working my nerves when I'm asleep.
Maybe it's the love that I'm fearing,
Or maybe I'm just a male chauvinistic narcissist
like my appearance.
Or maybe I'm too incoherent.
I hear it,
But it goes in one ear and out the other.
Maybe I get it from my mother
'cause we're like one another.
We're both suckers 4 pain
but can't explain where it comes from.
I wasn't prepared for this.
Maybe I inherited this suffering,
a deep-rooted, love-dysfunctional heritage.
Whatever it is — I love it.

The love, the pain, the chaos that comes from it.
Even when it makes me sick to my stomach,
I still stick to this loving.
I'm stuck with it.
I'd rather have it than have nothing.
I'll be okay regardless
'cause I pray every day,
And God's promise is my harness.

No Calls, No Mail

I went to jail, and in one week, you left me
left me weak, took my breath from me.
Now I can't even breathe,
'cause I never thought you would leave.

You left my messages on read,
And my tank on E.
Can't believe you left me
Got a blank on me, a mystery.

You were supposed to be my backbone,
But you were spineless,
broke up our unhappy home.
Loyalty is supposed to be timeless.

We could've worked it out
It wasn't that bad, truth be told,
I never knew you could be
that ruthless though.

I never cheated or deleted you,
the best is all I've ever seen in you.

Yeah, I got mental issues
But don't we all do?
You only loved me for the physical.

They say love is blind,
but I say out of sight, out of mind.
You didn't waste time finding another
to fill my void.
In my mind, you're still mine,
But I'm still annoyed.

I'm in my feelings,
can't believe you'd leave that fast
left me neglected.
Like Usher, I got it bad...
These are my confessions.

I was faithful and loyal to a fault.
I was broke, you made me pay attention
to everything that you bought.

I fell in love when I kissed you,
then skipped through to being with you.
Even with trust issues,

I still trusted you
but now look what you do.
When they put handcuffs on me,
I thought you'd hold it down.
Thanks for nothing.

Mysteriously, you found love
in someone else's company,
doing to him what you done to me.
You used to love me and hug me
I was addicted; you were like a drug to me.

Cold nights, you cuddled me,
Now I'm in jail, and you want nothing from me.
Not even friendship
Wow, I never knew
You could be this vindictive.

When I said I loved you, I meant it.
Now I see your reciprocation was senseless;
You just loved me by the minute, by the moment.
And I had my own home
to you, which was a bonus.

My mistakes? I own them.
But what about your crazy ways,
controlling?
I could've left but I stayed,
even with omens telling me, "Let her go."
I couldn't leave you homeless.

I never strayed from commitment,
but now I'm sick in a cell
with symptoms of sickle cell.
My heart is broken
the real case when I was sent to jail.
Now I'm hot, living in hell.
Can't see, can't feel, can't you tell?

I'm trying to be strong,
no phone calls, no emails, no letters in the mail.
I'm a mess,
I can't believe you cut me out of your life.
Your viciousness prevailed.

I can't believe you'd forget about me.
Now I'm alone.
They said love is a disease it fits the phrase

From love to hate, it's a phase.

Did I put you in that much dis-ease?

Is that bad for you to breeze?

Even Drew Brees stayed loyal to his team.

It wasn't that bad

I didn't get life,

I was coming right back

with my spine attached.

Now I'm sad, in jail, no bail,

alone with my thoughts.

I wish I could take it all back.

But for now,

I'll pray for a better day

to reverse the hurt

and get my heart back.

Sometimes the loudest silence is from the one who said they'd stay.

Sixth Inning Switch

I just wish you had said this at the beginning,
Now you're trying to switch up pitches
in the 6th inning,
Save the game for the lames,
Playing these tired games with borrowed names.

And unclick my pictures,
Delete the memories, erase the fixtures,
Try to figure out or reconfigure,

Then reconsider who was bigger.

I know the difference between sweet and bitter,
Tasted both enough to be no quitter,
It doesn't always mean it's gold because it glitters.
Sometimes diamonds hide among the litter.

You thought you'd change the rules mid-play,
Rewrite the story, and have it your way,
But I've been keeping score since the third day,
And truth doesn't fade, you're not here to stay.

So take your late apologies and revised edition,
I'm done accepting conditional admissions.
I know my worth, I made my decision,
Real recognizes real with ill precision.

The game was over when you switched your
stance,
You can't ask for a second first chance,
I peeped the difference at a glance:
What glitters ain't gold—it's just circumstance.

Not Worth It

I wish I had known better,
not to confuse your conversation with flirtation.
I guess you were just being cordial
out of courtesy for my reputation.
I hope my infatuation
would not be seen as an asphyxiation.
I was always told
that if I want something, I should go get it
because remorse can last for ages.
We spent nights pillow talking on the phone.
I guess I was just a source of entertainment
When you were lonely and alone.
That was dead wrong,
because you led me on.
I was thinking that one day
We were going to be a family,
But you spoon-fed me along.

"If you really wanted me,
or did you only want my company?"
It was the question that I didn't ask,
but the answer that I needed to know so bad.
You said that your heart was hurt in the past.
What does that have to do with me?

I didn't deserve this.

I always treated you like a queen,

But you seemed to treat me

as if I were your servant.

Let me know when your circumstances change

to me, it's worth the chances that I take,

even if I have to go through

All this hurt and the pain.

If you didn't want to be with me,

you should have told me,

instead of playing the fifty and holding me.

You were so phony.

You even consoled me when my pops died,

As I cried right by your side.

You would just ask sly

to get cash and rides on the side.

Maybe it was my pride,

But in my eyes,

You were my ride or die.

But you always had an excuse

to do what I liked.

You would let me caress you,

But never undress you.

And out of respect for you,

I would never pressure you

But what a finesse move.

I found it impossible to like you.

One minute, I wanted to make love to you,

but in the next minute, I wanted to fight you.

I've never seen anyone like you.

You would go from so succulent

to a cold bitch in a tight minute.

What a shiest move!

In hindsight, I can now see

That was just your defense mechanism.

You were out to get whatever you could get

from men.

I also heard

that you weren't even a virgin.

And you were only flirting with me

for monetary purposes.

You were only concerned

with your self-preservation and your earnings...

Now I'm hurting and deserted.

You weren't worth it.

Chapter 6: Unwavering

Faith through the storm—rebuilding identity and strength in God.

"The heart steadies, the soul aligns. Through trials and betrayals, faith becomes the anchor in our lives... standing firm, rising stronger, and refusing to break but still strive."

Unwavering

As I navigate through the remnants of your influence,
Stepping carefully through the debris,
Through shattered promises and broken trust,
I grapple with the aftermath of your deceit
Our love was just a bust.

Each lie a stone I must move aside,
Each manipulation is a path I must untangle.
The landscape you left behind
is treacherous; you finagled

Mined with doubt and seeded with shame,
But I am learning to read this terrain,
To recognize your traps for what they are,
To see the difference between afar

Your damage and my truth.
Despite the chaos you sowed,
The confusion you cultivated,
the troubles you provoked

The garden of self-doubt you tended in my mind,
I hold onto the belief that my worth
Transcends the narratives you painted for me.
With you, my life was in recline
Your story was never my scripture.

You tried to rewrite me,
To edit my essence,
To revise my reality until I became
A character in your fiction
Small enough to control,
Broken enough to need your convincing
Though stained and scarred by our interactions,
Bearing marks that may never fully fade,
I refuse to drown in the murky reflection
You cast upon me. I'm hurt and afraid
That distorted image in troubled waters
Was never who I am.
I will not become that person.
You tried to convince me I was.

I will not shrink to fit.
The diminished space you created.
I will not accept the labels.
You tried to brand upon my soul.
Too bad we didn't make it

Even as I confront my own imperfections and demons,
The genuine flaws that are mine to face,
The real work that calls me forward,
I know the difference now between my place

True accountability and your false accusations,
Between growth and your gaslighting.

I stand resilient as a child of God,
Rooted in something deeper than your opinions,
Anchored in a love you could not shake,
Held by hands you could not break

Unwavering in my inherent value.
This worth was woven into me
Before you arrived, boo
It will remain long after you're gone,
Cannot be diminished by your words,
It cannot be erased by your actions.
I am more than what happened to me.
I am more than how you treated me.
I am more than the worst moments
Of our shared history.
And today, I choose to believe.
What God says about me
Over what you said about me.

I am navigating forward,
Through the remnants,
Beyond the aftermath,
Toward wholeness.
without trembling
Scarred but standing.
Stained but sacred.
Imperfect but invaluable.
Unwavering.

Rising From the Ashes

The phone stays silent.
But I'm learning to speak to myself
Not the old me who needed validation,
But the man I'm becoming in this cell.

You left me in the darkness.
So I had to find my own light.
Started with a flicker,
A prayer in the middle of the night.

Then meditation at dawn,
Then words on a page,
Then the realization that I was born
To survive this cage.

I thought I needed you to make it.
Thought your voice was my lifeline.
But every unanswered call
Was teaching me to stand on my own spine.

You were my crutch.
And when you left, I had to learn to walk.
Now I'm running toward a future.
Where I don't need you to talk.

Twenty years hanging over my head,
98% conviction rate,
But I'm in that 2% mindset.
I refuse to accept this fate.
Not with bitterness,
Not with rage,
But with the clarity that comes
From being stripped down in the cage

I'm not the man who spent money to keep you close.
I'm not the man who needed your attention the most.
I'm becoming someone stronger.
Someone who can stand alone,
Someone who learned that home
Isn't there a person on the phone

It's the foundation I build with God.
Brick by brick, stone by stone.
You taught me what I didn't want to learn:
That's the only person I can count on.

It is the one I see when I look within.
So thank you for the abandonment.
Thank you for the pain.
Because it forced me to find myself again.

I still got 20 years of pressure.
Still got the feds breathing down my neck.
But I also got something they can't measure.
A spirit they can't break or wreck.

The phone might never answer.
You might never come back around.
But I'm rising from these ashes.
With or without you holding the crown

I'm learning hope isn't something someone gives you.
It's something you create in the dark.
And survival isn't just breathing.
It's finding your purpose, your path, your spark.

So let the phone stay ringing.
Let the visits never come from home.
I'm becoming who I was meant to be.
Not in spite of being alone,
But because of it.
I'm free in here.
More free than I ever was with you.
And when I walk out these doors,
I'll be brand new.

Child of God

As I navigate the remnants
of your influence,
I walk through ruins of trust,
grappling with the echoes
of your deceit.
As our love starts to rust
You sowed chaos
like seeds in tender soil,
and from them grew doubt
thorned and choking.
You wasnt loyal

Yet still, I breathe.
Still, I rise.
For my worth is not the portrait
you painted in your bitterness.
At night, I cried

Your words may have stained me,
But they did not define me.
I refuse to drown
in the murky reflection

you cast upon my name.
Get from around me

Even as I confront
my own imperfections,
my own quiet demons,
I stand—unshaken.
God was my protection.
For beneath the scars,
beneath the ache,
a sacred truth remains:
I am a child of God,
formed from light,
held by the mercy of His reign
And crowned with grace.
Though you tried
to silence my faith
I have learned to sing again
a psalm of healing,
a psalm of restoration.

I am still here.
Still, I'm whole.
Still, I'm His—soul.

Refined

I gotta refine myself to re-find myself,
to remind myself that I'm God's creation.
I need to redesign my health, define my self-wealth
'cause that's worth more than what I'm making.

It's vital to my survival,
'cause I'm tired of being lied to
by that ni**a in the mirror —
the one, who to my soul is a pyro.

He's my Dr. Jekyll,
trying to tear my hides from the inside,
smoking that potent potion,
with a high-content portion of formaldehyde.

They said we was born to die, evidently
but I'm trying to outlive the life expectancy
of a poverty-perverse kid, unexpectedly.

They expected me to be out here
toting guns and promoting drugs
but I need to change my habits like a nun.
I'm just an addict that needs love.

I'm really trying to be healthy,
but I feel like somebody put a spell on me,

'cause I keep sabotaging myself
so ain't no need to tell on me.
I'm a walking felony,
smoking dust L's like weed,
can't seem to excel or succeed.
I'll get sober from June to October,
then celebrate Halloween
with a bundle of anti-Jehovah.
and a bottle of lean

then I'll go to rehab,
then be back picking through my mental scabs,
then next thing I know,
I'm blowing shows with three bags.
Now I'm back on the ave,
pants sagging off my a$$,
tryna holler at thots
'cause I know they're gonna give it up fast.

Risking my life with bad decisions,
tripping up my Nikes,
messing up my checks
'cause my vision isn't right or with precision.

What is it that I like,
that I'd entertain something so strange,
something that's messing up my brain,
got me type skittish all night again?

Maybe I'm addicted to the strife and the pain,
maybe I'm dependent on the plights and the likes,
living my life in a crisis.
Maybe I just need Jesus Christ
Maybe I just need a psyche.
(I dunno.)

Maybe I need to get it right
from the same docs that judged me,
then prescribed me with contradictions
synthetic Percocets
that would've got me addicted
if I didn't know how to read it right.
The same ones typing up descriptions
to get me in tight predicaments,
misreading my rights

unjustly...
it ain't feasible or sufficed to me.
Or maybe I'm just crazy,
like how my ex wife made me to be
loving the chaos,
riding roller-coasters
that break me.
I can't shake the D's
demons, devils, depression,
demonic expressions.
For every progressive step,

there's three in regression.
I keep forgetting the consequences,
the jail sentences I endured
soon as I walk out them doors,
I just need one more.
But one ain't enough,
and two is too many.
I'm stuck in this psycho cycle,
draining all of my energy.
I need to take the 12 steps to recovery,
to rediscover me.
Before I can love someone else,
First I gotta love me.

So I must take the first step on this journey alone,
admit I have a problem,
that I'm powerless—'cause I'm grown.

Then I gotta take responsibility
for my past actions,
ask God and others for forgiveness,
then seek repentance.

I know this is a lifelong process,
a regimen, a testament in motion,
but Inshallah,
I'll make it far enough
to turn my scars into devotion.

Chapter 7: Deliverance

Breaking the chains — confronting the self, the system, and the spirit.

"Facing your demons, your past, and the world that tried to hold you down. Deliverance is raw, messy, and real designed. It;s a battle of spirit, mind, and body that leads to freedom of the mind."

Convicted to Affliction

Being convicted and addicted to afflictions
at a young age
kept me full of rage, but I came to love the pain.
It was the only thing that gave me meaning
and reasoning.
It also gave me motivation
to live through goals to achieve with.

But the worse it got,
I had to mask it to hide my symptoms.
The synthetic dopamine gave me hope,
but the addiction was getting more vicious.
I am both the poison and the antidote,
destroying what I was building.

I would make illogical posts.
When I was high on smoke.
I couldn't cope.
My friends stayed at a distance.
They started ignoring me,
not even acknowledging my existence.
It was me that was the problem,

But I was pointing fingers,
blaming everything else for the enigma
while my problems were getting bigger and bigger.

It was as if I wasn't in a fight, a debate,
or another chaotic situation,
It didn't feel right or was faked.
I was prone to a predicament
That was filled with melancholy.
I was always getting into it,
and my felonies would unjustly follow me,
even though afterward
I would offer broad but sincere apologies.
I really mean what I say,
But the pain takes me away with anomalies.

Behind the scenes,
I'm a self-slayer and a drama king.
I-G is not my reality.
I have five felonies and an addictive personality,
So please don't follow me.

I'm also addicted to and intend
on soliciting ghetto-beautiful women.

Arguments are normal.
Domestic violence is a mutual rendition.
I can't even begin to explain,
But it seems like my whole environment
is addicted to the pain.
I am just a product of it.
I'm one of them.

Pain is probably the only thing besides cain
That would numb the brain.
Prodigality, we prospered by design, or was it
ordained?
I don't know,
But according to how I was trained,
I was taught to persevere through my worst fear
like a runaway train.
To others, it may seem insane,
but to us, it was simple and plain.
We reverse the hurt and bond with the pain.

My Own Worst Enemy

Is it just me,
or do I seem to subconsciously love to hate myself?
I do things to sabotage my visage, to degrade myself.
I look at a distorted mirage,
a reflection of when I betray my health.
Afraid of help, which leads me to being
often caged and shelved.

It was me that put that poison of self-defeat
in my inner being.

Somehow, along this lifelong journey,
I became my own worst enemy.
I wasn't into myself.
I was more worried about all the wrong things,
such as intimacy.
The women I would see,
I would plead for their love and their sympathy.

Physically, I was deteriorating and infuriated
that I couldn't find a quick fix.
All my mind was on, was getting chicks.
I took explicit pictures for thirst traps to work those
apps,
But I had nothing to add to their life but hurt and wrath.

I was taking late-night bird baths on random dirt paths,
passed out on the love boat,
Then the next day I'm in church taking naps.
Not only have I seen the image of God,
but also of the devil.
When I looked in the mirror,
I could hardly escape that rebel.

Intoxication...
which often led me to the boxes or hospitalizations.
Addictions are hard to stop it.

I came to a surreal realization.
My sister found me butt-naked
on the pavement with a twisted face.
My so-called friends were recording me,
taking pictures for clickbait.

They were embarrassing me,
just to laugh at me casually.
I needed to quit, but I have to do it gradually.
The pain I intended to relieve would never leave.
It was just masked.
It just multiplied and always came back to me
even more than before I conceived.

I was reversing the benefits.
I had injuries to my limbs and ligaments,
putting myself in a dangerous predicament.
I always claimed to be innocent,
but when is this going to end?
I'm always playing on defense.
There goes my sobriety in the wind.
I blamed everybody, never blamed myself,
But in reality, what I really needed was some help.

Caged by Deception

Full of venom, madly lying.

Had me trapped like a mad lion.

Roaring behind iron bars, soul is slowly dying.

But thank God for DNA strands and science.

And a lawyer whose pressure kept applying.

For his indigent client, that was barely surviving.

The truth cracked the cage and set me free.

But I still carry the scars mentally, silently.

I could have been doing two to twenty-three.

False accusations painting me as a beast permanently,

Because one woman weaponized the law viciously,

Try to assassinate my peace strategically.

She wore a mask—a Mona Lisa deceit.

A masterpiece of manipulation, emotionally elite.
Had my mind hemorrhaging on repeat.
She had me chain-smoking, stressed in the streets.
She was married to Keith, entangled in sheets.
Dragging me through adultery's defeat.

I kicked her out, severed the ties.
Then cops came around under moonlit skies.
Blue lights bounced like fireflies.
They said "DV," from an old rap sheet's lies,

I was arrested, tested, and my spirit was oppressed.
All over fabrications that she confessed.
Said it was rage, emotions compressive,
The sex was consensual, never forced or aggressive.
But she was lying, strategically obsessive.
Just trying to "teach me a lesson" is excessive.

Six weeks gone—a man caged by deception's art,
A modern-day lynching without leaving a mark.
But God knows my heart beats in the light, not the dark.
I would never hurt a woman—that's not my spark.
Now I move like a monk—spiritual but intentional.
Left her before things got critical and delusional.

I love God more than pain or pleasure's potential,
And I'm guarding my purpose like it's presidential.

So here is my testimony, my parting decree:
Stop calling the cops when your lover's unfaithful,
let it be.
Call for peace, not police—dial serenity.
If it's hands that harm you, fists flying violently,
Then protect your peace and move decisively.
But don't misuse the law for revenge so greedily.
False charges cut deeper than surgical sheaves.

Where love becomes evidence and trust decays.
Stop weaponizing the flaws embedded in legal parades,
Learn to heal your wounds, not wage crusades.
Staying in toxicity is worse than the pain that fades.
Leave the battlefield before you become the grenade.
Do it for the cause, for the lives that can be saved.
Do it for the truth that refuses to be enslaved.
Do it for yourself and never be afraid.

Domestic terrorists

Frivolous charges of domestic violence.
The new way to silence women and men.
They misuse the flaws in the law.
Dragging us back into court again and again.
When does this nonsense end?
They pitted us against each other.
Transform our homes into battle zones.
Keeping us from thriving.
Dividing the family, erasing the tone.

I know some men who are violent.
Wild and downright cowardice
But those aren't the ones they call the cops on.
Funny how that pattern is.
One small argument, one bad night.
And now, blue lights flash bright.
The family split.
Court dates hit.
CPS knocking like thieves in the crib.

Now, it's double orders of protection.
A parent can't see their kid's reflection.
Two people lost in deception.
Confused by emotion's infection.

All over a fuse that someone blew,
But who knew the law would measure it too?
If it doesn't apply, let it fly.
but I have seen women get punched in the eye.
Call the cops.
Then the next day, they had lunch with the guy.
That dude's wrong; I won't defend it.
Violence doesn't get no credit.
And men that hit women might deserve to die.
But I've seen others cry fake tears.
Plot revenge, play fears.
Calling the police to destroy careers.

Now he is stuck in the beast's belly.
Weeks and weeks in concrete valleys.
And when he finally gets free,
They got right back together instantly—insanity.

Love is blind.
But the system looks fine.
Every tear, every lie, every signature line.
The same judge is stamping orders.
That keeps fathers from their sons.
And nobody wins when revenge begins.
It just ruins everything for everyone.

No Third Party

Hey, baby, can you forgive me?
For acting crazy?
I'm locked up for conspiracy,
And they're trying to give me a century.
This ain't me!
Please forgive me,
I may be a lot of things,
But I'm not fugazi.
I thought you were trying to play me
My bad, baby.

Next time, come directly to me
If you've got something to say,
Because by the time the message gets to me,
It's all distorted anyway.

It kinda affected me
The way you disrespected me,
The way it was told to me.
I laid back and replayed our conversations,
Reread your letters.
Couldn't find one reason
Why would you come at me like that—never.
But I should've known better,
Because that didn't sound like you,
It sounded more like the people

That surrounds you, boo.
It's cool, nobody's perfect
If I was you, I'd pursue myself too,
Because I know I'm worth it.

I'm sorry to hear you're having issues with your family,
I understand it—see,
I'm here to steer you back to sanity.
That's the Godly man in me.
To lend a helping hand where needed,
I get my blessings
As my faith in Almighty God is deepened.

I'm here for you, got an ear for you,
I'll be there for you.
In a place that's hard to find grace,
I still care for you.
Good guys do exist
I'll bear with you,
Be sincere with you, yeah, you!
But be careful
Don't let the devil grasp and trap you,
Have you acting out of character,
Like a flat note.
And I wasn't trying to carry you
Like an addict,
But I gave my Cash App,
Just in case—you can have it.

You asked for it!
Baby, why didn't you dedicate your time?
To tell me you don't like me,
And I had to hear it
From my main man's wifey?
That's spicy.

We have to have better communication,
I'll be patiently in my room pacing,
Waiting for you to pull up.
But I don't think they even really told you,
That's why I am "in my bag" when I scold you.

Because my drive is money,
And I'm trying to invest it in you.
Being real and true
It is the best I can do.
If you didn't hear it from my mouth,
Then I didn't say it.
Stop letting people use my statements
When I never okayed it!
I don't need a third party or an assistant pimp.
Miss,
Give me them lips for a sincere goodnight kiss.
I'll holler at you tomorrow,
We can start a new slate.
It's us, never them
Yours forever, my boo mate.

164

Raft in the Ocean

I swear to God that it's hard to focus.
One minute I'm confident,
Next, I'm feeling hopeless,
Like a raft in the ocean.

I act before I think
and move mostly off of emotions.
Perhaps I'm going to sink
and lose all of my promotions.
I need to make atonement.

I inadvertently denied the signs
by the way of the Owens,
knowing that the end of my days
They are quickly approaching.

The love of money is the root of all evil,
And I was working for the devil.
Hitting ditches in the road to the riches,
putting the pedal to the metal.

It took me 3,000 days

for me to change my situation profoundly.
I went through separation from my family
and isolation from humanity.
I needed a strong drink of humility
and a dozen humble pies.
My psyche and I
haven't been seeing eye to eye.
I sabotaged my own life.

I was on my knees
asking God to forgive me sincerely,
But then, when I got back in the streets,
I was doing things that impaired me.

My way of thinking was backwards and twisted,
valuing the false positives
over my subsequent consequences.
I have been neglected and abandoned since birth
only led me to self-hate.
Now my health is at stake.

The more I got older,
The more of my body the pain took control of
my fate.

I got to a point where I thought that I was hurting,
But it was just a false premonition
to make it seem like relief was worth it.

The worst is that I couldn't blame anyone else
When I sabotaged myself.
I was caught up in the mirage of pleasure and
wealth.

The lessons were sent on the ball,
But I ignored them all.
The Psalms in my palm said,
"Price comes by the fall."
Pause.

I gotta thank the Lord
for watching over me
and for protecting me.
I used to be my worst enemy.
My negative urges infected me.
It reflected on me negatively,
but not once did He neglect me.
He accepted me for who I am...
one of His images, allegedly.

Chapter 8: Revolving Doors

Closure, reflection, and quiet victory—the calm after the storm.

"The storm passes. Scars remain, but the heart breathes easy. This chapter is about renewal, gratitude, and finally blooming where pain once rooted me."

Revolving whore/door

Part I: Confusion

I don't know why I keep ending up

with these different females

that appear to be my blessings.

Then when we argue,

they seem to leave me with aggression.

I never seem to get it

or learn from the lessons.

I keep forgetting to second-guess

their intentions and rhetorics,

and not pay attention to my six senses

and my intuition

until it's prophetic.

I'm pathetic...

I was never good at listening

because I was too concerned

with their retention of acceptance.

Part II: The Fall

My ex, whose name I won't forget to mention,

only loved me in the beginning.
She was a thot
that was into reading tarot cards
but folded when my pockets started thinning.
She was grinning when we were winning.

Then eventually, mentally,
she was out of here like a dandruff conditioning.

At first, it was the distancing.
Then she started acting indifferently
flaky like a pastry.

She said she loved me
but showed me that she really hated me,
making me crazy when she was being fugazi.
Her attitude and actions were like a laxative:
sh!tty and shady.

Looking back at it,
she was simping me simply and brazenly.
But I was in love with her crazily,
like Beyoncé and Jay-Z, dangerously.
I was gifting her amazingly.

I took out all types of debts
to alphabet on her from A to Z,
just for her to play me
and pay me with greed distastefully.
Then she got bitter at a nigga
when I sent her to free agency.
I needed to put her to the rear,
but I thought she would be sincere.
My vision was impaired by complacency.

Part III: The Revelation

Since we've been unpaired,
I rarely get to see her here,
since she started acting weird
with her infrequencies.
She was acting like I wasn't even there
when she sees me.
She would just stare in a state of mind,
or as if she was blind,
as if she was Stevie.

I wonder if she even cares about me,
or is just wasting my time
like a broke stolen Rollie,

just to flex on me with great complexity.
It isn't fair,
and I hate that I'm even compared
to her other exes,
past and presently.

But I guess she didn't know
that I had the passcodes to her phone
and saw those illicit texts last week
when she was in Texas with them creeps,
receiving d!ck pics and texting back recklessly,
sending nudes and pubes
like she didn't have a dude effortlessly.
She was an embarrassment to my presence
with her insecurities and inefficiencies.

Yes, I'm a special breed.
She swept me from under my feet
when she slept with me,
but what I didn't see
was that I was sleeping with a snake,
definitely indefinitely.

She would always leave a trace of her reverberates

when she tried to inconspicuously
answer her phone next to me,
which was on vibrate,
which we both hated conceptually.
I guessed her sexual vibration elations
turned into an evasion of me perpetually.

Am I just supposed to be okay with this?
I'd rather die being a mental patient impatiently
with an open wrist.

Part IV: Reflection

To be honest, I am trying to cope with this
by ignoring the topic of her being topless,
underneath another man riding his sausage.

But somehow I gotta get my pride
and my heart fixed
before it's forever tarnished.
Pardon my riffs!

But what I don't understand or get
is this vomit that I keep returning to.
Maybe it's the dog in me,

or the karma keeping me vulnerable.
Somehow I keep going through
the same revolving door of whores,
but maybe it's me
attracting how I used to be
all along before.
I can't complain,
because when you pray for love and change,
you have to expect the mud with the rain.
Meanwhile, I keep gargling this damned
champagne.
As I inspect and then ingest this pain
that I'm a sucker for,
I have to, in retrospect, correct all of my wrongs.

I need to learn from those burns
so I won't have to turn to—or return to
a female for love,
just for me to get an urn in return.
Duh!

I was just a prince crying like a dove.
It is what it is.
It was what it was.

Part V: Redemption
But first, I need to pray,
then make way for me
to love myself second to the Lord.
Then be honest and just trust in His process
and stop messing around with all those whores
which includes myself.

I need some help that I never got before.
Then I need to find confidence and strength
within me
and stop looking to everyone else to help,
which I abhor.
Then close the doors
so they won't keep revolving on and on.

Then work on solutions
rather than my problems or the causes
so I can carry on.

My word is my bond,
and the Lord made me strong
to endure the war that I tarry on.

So I'm going to trust in this process
and strive not to return to the vomit like a dog.

Her name was Missus Pain,
whose sister was Karma
whom I was involved with
in some type of ménage à trois.
Their husbands were bugging,
but not for nothing, I was wrong.
So I must change
or remain in this same game
that I keep repeating,
which has had me torn.

I'm going to strive
and take it one day at a time
until I see the sun shine through the storm…

I'm gone.

999th Attempt

You got me stalking you
just to talk to you.
Where did we go wrong?
I need answers and justification
just to move on.

I'm torn. I'm lost.
I don't know what I could have done better.
I could have sworn I treated you well,
but your actions were like,
"Well... whatever."

If ever you want to talk
and come back home to the house again,
we can work it out through counseling
just don't bounce again.

Whatever I have to do
to get my boo back, I will do.
My heart is bruised by depression.
I'm confused by your aggression.
This isn't you...

You're not the same woman I met
and slept with after our first date.
We were inseparable,
so it's unacceptable
for you to ghost me like Lorenzo Tate.

Even as I hesitate
to go by your new man's place,
my patience flaked.
I needed to see your face;
I couldn't let it wait.

I stayed awake; I couldn't sleep.
My heart and my head ached.
I was feeling like dead weight,
smelling like sour red grapes.

I need your Kodak smile with this whine.
I'm on my knees this time,
begging for another chance for romance,
because I need you in my life.
Unconditional love is how I found the strength.

This is now my 999th attempt,

hoping that my persistence
will overcome your resistance.
Whatever we did, we did it—it's done!
I forgive you.
Let's continue and start over from day one,
when I kissed you.

It was bad, but we both did our dirt.
You were a flirt, I was a "hoe,"
but what we had was worth more than gold.

So... let bygones be bygones.
Come back home.
I'm so tired of being alone.
At least you can answer the phone.

The 1000th Truth

I deleted your number after attempt 999. Realized I was drowning, trying to throw you a line. You never wanted saving, never wanted me at all. I was just background music, while you waited for his call.

I blamed myself for everything, thought I could fix the break, But some things ain't meant for mending—some love is just a fake. You had me on my knees while you were laughing with your friends,I was writing you love letters while you plotted out my end.

I drove by your place one last time, but I didn't stop the car. Finally understood that closure comes from who you are. Not from apologies you'll never get or answers they won't give... The real question isn't why they left, it's why I wouldn't live.

My reflection told me something that my heart refused to hear: "You can't love someone into loving you, that much is clear." I was begging for the crumbs while there's a table set for me, Somewhere out there, someone's praying for the love I give for free.

So this is my 1000th attempt — but this time it's for me, To choose myself, to love myself, to finally break away free. No more stalking past your window, no more hitting up your phone. The strongest thing I ever did was learning that I'm not alone.

This ain't about forgiveness or forgetting what went down, It's about me picking up my crown up off the ground. You taught me what I'll never be—and that's somebody's maybe. The next person gets my best: a real man, not just a watcher for your babies.

Thank You for The Pain

I let my guard down
and trusted you.
You said you needed me,
but weeded me,
then depleted me.

Thanks for the lessons you showed me
they molded me.
I'm aware, I'm prepared now,
yeah, you scolded me.
But still...

I thank you.

Don't hate you.

Won't break you.

I'm gonna do whatever it takes to improve.

God saw me through it,

used it to strengthen me,

gave me my faith back

all the way from Calvary.

Thank you for the pain

that you caused me.

It grew me,

renewed me,

and softened me.

I'm not bitter

I'm better.

I smile bigger now.

God saw me through this

My vision's clearer now.

I see purpose

in the pieces that fell apart.

I see healing

where there used to be scars.
You thought you broke me,
but you built my heart.

I was blind to my worth,
but now I see
I was never lost,
God was leading me.

So I rise...
rooted,
refined,
redeemed.
I rise from what once
was a shattered dream.
You were the storm,
but I was the seed.
And God
He watered me.

Now I bloom.
Now I breathe.
Now I believe.

About Author

Coolgmack is a voice forged in the concrete jungles of Westchester and NYC, a poet who turned pain into purpose. After graduating from Sleepy Hollow High, his path led him through Rikers Island, an experience that sharpened his words into weapons of truth.

Though he is still serving an unjust, perpetual sentence from a crime committed 20 years ago that carried only a 10-year term, Coolgmack does not let that deter him. From behind bars, he channels the grit of survival and the ache of injustice into his work.

Poetry remains his sanctuary, his megaphone, and his redemption, fueling his fight against injustices in Amerikkka. Coolgmack is an author, publisher, and entrepreneur on a mission to spark a revolution through revelation, helping communities uncover their inner strength. His latest work, including "poetic injustices in Amerikkka," is a testament to the holy fusion of pain, passion, and purpose.

Find him everywhere the ink spills—on all social media platforms, including TikTok, YouTube, Twitter, and Instagram, where he is universally known as @coolgmack, or visit his website at coolgmack.com.

More books by Coolgmack

Find all these titles on all book platforms and coolgmack.com

"POETIC INJUSTICE$ IN AMERIKKKA" by Coolgmack is a powerful lyrical analysis of systemic racism in America. This thought-provoking work provides firsthand insight into institutional racism while advocating for economic and social restitution for Black Americans. examines historical oppression and its impact on current socioeconomic structures, race relations, and politics. He argues for changing the rules of economic opportunity so everyone has a fair chance to succeed. Drawing from multigenerational community experiences, he passes down ancestral wisdom and survival strategies, reminding his people they are enough and encouraging them to choose life beyond pain and trauma.

offers a raw and unfiltered look at the complexities of love. In this powerful collection, he navigates the tumultuous journey from **heartbreak and betrayal** unwavering pursuit of a love that is true and lasting.

Sucker4Love is a testament to the pain and triumph of human connection. With a voice that is both vulnerable and resilient, Coolgmack exposes the deep scars of past relationships while holding onto the hope for a future defined by genuine intimacy and devotion.

This is a book for anyone who has ever been a **"sucker for love"**—who has given their all and lost, only to rise again with a stronger belief in the power of an honest heart

Sucker4love Too: "Love Ain't Logical its lyrical" is a soul-baring collection of poetry from coolgmack that navigates the intricate dance of love, loss, and self-discovery. The author invites you into his world, where heartfelt verses are a testament to his journey. He grapples with the absence of a father he never knew while finding guidance in his spiritual legacy. He confronts past mistakes and addiction, offering a profound apology to his mother that resonates with raw honesty. The collection delves deep into the tumultuous landscape of romantic love—from the dizzying highs of a "flawless" romance to the agonizing lows of a broken heart. Through poems that are both vulnerable and resilient, the author explores the challenges of trusting again and the hope that persists even after disappointment. Sucker4love Too is more than just poetry; it's a powerful narrative of resilience, a tribute to the enduring power of love, and a beacon for anyone seeking to find their way back to themselves.

Psalms in My Palms is a collection of heartfelt psalms, prayers, and poetic reflections born out of seasons of pain, redemption, and unshakable faith. Drawing from his personal journey through hardship, incarceration, and spiritual renewal, Coolgmack—offers words that meet readers in their darkest valleys and guide them toward God's light. Each piece blends lyrical beauty with scriptural truth, speaking to those who feel broken, oppressed, or forgotten. Within these pages are declarations of gratitude, prayers for strength and deliverance, and poetic portraits of God's unchanging love.

More than a book of poems, this is a devotional companion—a sacred space where you can pause, reflect, and write your own prayers in response. Psalms in My Palms is for anyone longing to be reminded that they are seen, chosen, and never alone. Whether rejoicing on the mountaintop or enduring a storm, you'll find words here to anchor your heart and lift your spirit.

Chronicles of a Hangry Black Soul is a raw, unapologetic poetry collection documenting a life hungry for truth, justice, and spiritual liberation. Through unfiltered verses, the author confronts systemic injustice, personal struggle, and the journey toward healing.The collection explores: **Social & Spiritual Commentary**: Exposing "rigged" world of scams and fake love while offering a mirror for self-discovery and a guide through modern chaos. **The Prison System**: Raw testimony of dehumanization and isolation, where freedom is elusive and the system reduces public defenders to jokes.**Relationships & Loyalty**: Examining betrayal by fair-weather friends and celebrating the "Day Ones" who remained loyal through adversity. **Healing & Transformation**: Chronicling evolution from the "drug game" to "Elevation Season"—rising spiritually, mentally, and financially to build a new kingdom with divine wisdom.

Sucker4drugs chronicles the journey through addiction, despair, and recovery, exploring substance abuse, violence, incarceration, and redemption through raw street experiences. The **Destructive Cycle** Early poems depict the devastating effects of drug use, particularly PCP. Characters like "Dirty Diana" and "Derek" illustrate addiction's physical and emotional toll—paranoia, violence, incarceration, and betrayal..**Personal Struggle** Poems delve into loneliness, desperation, and internal conflict, portraying the relentless grip drugs have on mind and spirit. Recovery **and Hope** Amidst darkness, the collection offers messages of hope, encouraging honesty, faith, and spiritual growth as tools for healing. The **Healing Journey** The "Day One" through "Day 28" series intimately documents recovery's daily struggles—confronting temptation, rebuilding life, and finding resilience.**Identity and Purpose** Poems explore self-discovery and reclaiming purpose, emphasizing that circumstances refine rather than define us.

They say love doesn't cost a thing—but for him, it costs everything. Sucker4Pain is a gritty, uncut testimony from a man who gave his all to the wrong women and nearly lost himself in the process. This ain't no love story—it's a survival story. Its raw pain served cold, dressed in designer lies and false promises. Through a poetic fusion of heartbreak, prison reflections, betrayal, addiction, and faith, this powerful collection gives voice to everyone who's ever been played, betrayed, locked up, or left behind. Told in vivid street verses and emotional confessionals, this book is more than poetry—it's a purge. A spiritual detox from toxic love and generational curses. From being set up and stripped down, to finding strength in the ruins, Sucker4Pain captures the real-life struggle of trusting the wrong women and finding God on the other side of grief.If you've ever been hurt, hustled, or hardened by love—you'll feel this in your soul.

Sucker4Lust is a collection of erotic poetry that delves into the raw, uninhibited world of desire and passion. The book is a journey through lust, presented through two distinct perspectives—that of a young, confident man consumed by his hunger, and women drawn to his intense charisma. The poems, which are at times witty, provocative, and tender, follow a narrative arc. They begin with an introduction to a world where lust is not a sin but a form of salvation. The stories then unfold through   the eyes of a character known as "Mr. Thriller," a seductive and unapologetic figure who navigates his desires with a captivating swagger. His verses are direct and sensual, celebrating the thrill of a physical connection. The collection also includes a female point of view, exploring the intoxicating pull of this "magnetic space" and the surrender to a "willing death" of passion. The book concludes with an "Aftermath" section, where the focus shifts from a purely physical connection to a deeper, more lasting bond, suggesting that lust, when fully explored, can evolve into something more profound. Ultimately, Sucker4Lust is a poetic exploration of the body's truth and the soul's temptation.

This unique collection of poetry is a walk in the world of SlowMotion.the author/poet Relatable situations. Loving words. Takes you to a place of a hurting heart, overcoming pain. Bravery and boldness to rebuild. Poems about Mending Hearts. Coming together and finding understanding.I'm excited for the world to read my words.I want to show the world that it is possible to live out your wonderful dreams positively. Keep dreaming Big

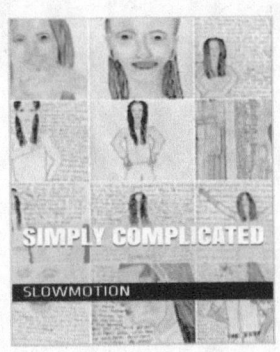

..This unique collection of poetry is a walk in the world of SlowMotion.Relatable situations.Loving words. Takes you to a place of a hurting heart, overcoming pain. Bravery and boldness to rebuild. Poems about Mending Hearts. Coming together and finding understanding

Psalms in My Palm 2 is a modern book of psalms — a lyrical testament of faith forged in fire. Through poetry, prayer, and spiritual reflection, the author walks the reader through a journey from pain to purpose, sin to surrender, and darkness to divine light. Each poem is both a confession and a revelation — spoken from the soul of a believer wrestling with real-life trials: incarceration, temptation, addiction, loss, and redemption. The voice is raw, unfiltered, yet deeply reverent. Like David's psalms reborn in a modern world, these verses echo both anguish and adoration, questioning and conviction. Across nine thematic chapters, the collection flows like scripture through the seasons of the human spirit: Morning and Purpose opens with gratitude and divine awakening. Repentance and Redemption confronts sin, guilt, and the courage to change. Faith in Adversity explores the endurance of the soul when surrounded by despair. Renewal and Transformation testifies to the rebirth that follows surrender. The Word and Wisdom honors the eternal guidance of scripture. Realization and Revival warns against false idols and celebrates awakening faith. Lament and Deliverance pours out the pain of injustice, isolation, and prayerful endurance. Praise and Gratitude restores peace through worship and thanksgiving. Salvation and Service closes with grace, purpose, and the calling to uplift others. Together, these psalms tell one continuous story — of a soul refined by struggle and redeemed by grace. It is a handbook for those seeking spiritual strength in hard times, a poetic ministry for anyone learning to walk again in the light of God.

Be$afe: The Illusion of Freedom is a poetic manifesto for the misunderstood, the incarcerated, the betrayed, and the reborn. In this searing collection, Coolgmack blends street wisdom, spiritual insight, and lyrical fire to expose the hidden costs of survival in Amerikkka. From prison cells to prayer closets, from fake friends to divine revelations, each chapter is a journey through pain, protest, and personal transformation. Through six chapters, author Coolgmack confronts the illusion of safety and support that often masks control and conditional generosity. He explores themes of betrayal by "frenemies" and the constant vigilance required for self-preservation, arguing that independence is the only real wealth. From the pain and isolation of being "behind bars" to the struggle of "The Square Life" and the journey of "The Rebuild", this work serves as both a confession and a manifesto. It is proof that freedom starts in the mind, faith starts in the heart, and change starts with the pen.

Poetic injustices in Amerikkka vol. 2

Justice Denied, Versified

Coolgmack

Poetic Injustices in Amerikkka: "Justice Denied, Versified" is Coolgmack's raw, unflinching spoken-word manifesto confronting **systemic oppression** and survival struggles within Black and Brown communities.

Drawing on his lived experience in "Killadelphia," Yonkers, and the prison-industrial complex, Coolgmack delivers a visceral social commentary across six thematic chapters that expose mass incarceration, police brutality, gentrification, and health disparities. This collection serves as both a **documentary in verse** and a powerful message of **resilience, self-awareness, and revolutionary resistance** for those ready to rise through the smoke and reclaim their narrative.

www.ingramcontent.com/pod-product-compliance
Lightning Source LLC
Chambersburg PA
CBHW010938120626
46554CB00008B/2522